A FATAL OBSESSION

By the same author

Non-fiction

Last Sunset
Miracle of Deliverance
Capturing Enigma

Novels

A Necessary End
Live Till Tomorrow

A FATAL OBSESSION

The Women at Cho Oyu – A Reporting Saga

Stephen Harper

Book Guild Publishing
Sussex, England

First published in Great Britain in 2007 by
The Book Guild Ltd
Pavilion View
19 New Road
Brighton, BN1 1UF

Typesetting in Times by
Acorn Bookwork Ltd, Salisbury, Wiltshire

Printed in Great Britain by
CPI Bath

A catalogue record for this book is available from
The British Library.

ISBN 978 1 84624 118 5

'I felt myself boiling with impotent rage, ready to dare anything if we could continue with the struggle. Although my reason saw it was the only logical decision to take, my heart refused to accept it. I didn't wish to bow my head before the wind and snow that must eventually hurl us back. "Don't turn back yet" I gasped.'

The leading French mountaineer, Claude Kogan, writing of her anger at her male expedition leader's decision to turn back in their attempt to reach the summit of Cho Oyu in 1954, five years before she led an all-woman expedition and died on the same mountain.

Contents

Foreword

I was thrilled to read this account of the women's international expedition to Cho Oyu well over 40 years ago. It had become very distant in my mind and such memories I had were always dominated by tragedy. The draft of the book inspired me to read my diary for the first time since I wrote it and this brought back vivid memories, allowing me to really identify with all that took place and appreciate my active involvement.

I am glad the tale is told as seen through the eyes of the man who was there. I don't think any of us properly realised the repercussions of our failure to co-operate fully. Stephen Harper was allocated to the expedition by the *Daily Express* which was providing considerable sponsorship. The *Express* had always hoped that he would accompany the expedition throughout from Kathmandu to the mountain. This was not acceptable to the leader Claude Kogan and to many of the members, and as a result there was a real lack of co-operation. It would be right to say that we did not entirely trust the *Daily Express*, being afraid they would sensationalise anything which took place. It is possible that the leader herself wanted to avoid any accusation that the expedition was relying on men, though in fact this was a difficult thing to sustain in view of the role of Sherpas and porters. The arrangement we tried to set up was that we should write daily diaries in duplicate, a copy to be sent back to the reporter who would remain in Kathmandu. That this is not how it worked out is very much the subject of this book and makes it much more than a simple report of a failed mountaineering expedition.

Seen from today's perspective of mountaineering it may seem surprising that it should be thought necessary to have an all-women's expedition, but in the 1950s so few women had ever climbed in the Himalayas that this was the only way of ensuring ordinary women could have the opportunity. Before the 1959 Cho Oyu expedition, Monica Jackson, Evelyn Camrass and Elizabeth Stark, as a party of just three women climbing in the Jugal Himal, made successful ascents of previously unclimbed mountains of 20,000 feet. A year after that I was a member of the Abinger

Himalayan expedition in which four British women under the leadership of Joyce Dunsheath succeeded in climbing mountains of similar height. The women's parties relied heavily on male porters and Sherpas, but so did all expeditions at that time. Tenzing's two daughters and his niece were members of the Cho Oyu party and they showed great promise as mountaineers as might have been expected. No doubt Sherpa women could be trained to be mountain guides and certainly Sherpanis made up a fair proportion of our porters from Namche Bazar to Base Camp, going over the Nangpa La Pass at 20,000 feet, but in 1959 it would not have been possible to do without male support.

Despite the tragedy and failure of this expedition, many women have since had great success in the Himalayas and other mountain ranges. Every year women are climbing all over the world. The Pinnacle Club, an all-women's British climbing club of which I am still a member, publishes a journal at two-yearly intervals. A recent edition has reports of seven expeditions to mountain ranges outside Europe.

In 1989 an all-women's team from Britain led by Rhona Lampard climbed Gasherbrums 11, a peak of 8,035 metres (26,360 feet). So 30 years passed before Claude Kogan's ambition to lead an all-women ascent of an 8,000-metre peak was realised.

For me there is no doubt that women now play their full part in mountaineering, and that is as it should be. The Cho Oyu expedition is properly part of the history of women's endeavours in mountains and I feel indebted to the author for ensuring that it should be.

Eileen Healey,
one of three British members of the 1959
Expédition Féminine au Nepal

Introduction

The allure of mountain climbing began in the last quarter of the eighteenth century when botanists began to explore the Alps for new plant specimens. Mont Blanc (15,774 feet, 4,807 metres), the highest peak in Europe west of the Caucasus, was first climbed in 1786 by Dr N.G. Paccard with Jacques Balmar, a pioneer Alpine guide. In 1838 the first woman to reach the summit of Mont Blanc was Mlle Henrietta d'Angeville, climbing with male guides in 1838, and in 1854 a Mrs Hamilton became the first British woman to follow her, climbing with her husband and guides. An English woman, Lucy Walker, was the first woman to scale the Matterhorn three years later. She became president of the Ladies Alpine Club when it was founded in 1907.

The Himalayas was regarded as a male preserve for some 60 years before Claude Kogan's Expédition Féminine 1959 au Nepal, just six years after members of an all-male British expedition climbed the 29,028-foot summit of Everest for the first time, a culmination of decades of effort to reach the summit of the world's highest mountain (see Appendix One). In the summer of 1959 Madame Claude Kogan, designer of chic beachwear in the Mediterranean resort of Nice, led an international team of 12 women, three of them from Britain, to Nepal with the aim of scaling Cho Oyu, a 26,750-foot peak in the Everest region, the sixth-highest mountain in the world. Several women, including two English women, have since stood on the Everest summit, on top of the world (see Appendix Two.)

At the time of the 1959 all-women Himalayan expedition, nobody could have envisaged women filling roles as front-line soldiers and jet pilots, or commanding a Royal Navy warship. The few women war correspondents became celebrities. Although a woman had climbed Mont Blanc more than a century before, the idea of women setting off to climb one of the highest Himalayan peaks, without male companions taking charge, was sensational.

PART ONE

Chapter One

A Dream Assignment

After retiring after a long career as a foreign correspondent I came across a unique archive, forgotten for decades while I was reporting wars, disasters and international politics around the world. Bundles of letters and notes sent to me decades before by members of the all-women Himalayan expedition along with photographs I had taken of this forgotten women's feat in attempting to scale a major Himalayan peak without the usual male companions and leadership. My inquiries showed that no full record of this extraordinary endeavour had ever been published, a sad omission from mountaineering history. This book is an attempt to fill that gap.

When the editor of the *Daily Express*, Arthur Christiansen, assigned me to cover the 1959 all-women expedition to the Himalayas, the prospect delighted me. Polar exploration and mountains had fascinated me since boyhood. The *Daily Express* had a special interest in the expedition along with the French magazine *Paris-Match* – they both contributed funds to the expedition, and expected a return.

Before becoming a foreign correspondent I had specialised in exploration and mountaineering and had been elected a Fellow of the Royal Geographical Society. Also, as a recent New Delhi correspondent, I had been among the first journalists ever allowed to enter Nepal when King Mahendra was crowned three years before. Until the end of British rule in India in 1947, only Britain had an Embassy in the Nepalese capital of Kathmandu, and till the coronation only a few foreigners, mainly members of climbing expeditions, had been allowed into the country.

My initial enthusiasm dipped when I discovered that the women expected me to cover their story from Kathmandu, basing my despatches on messages they promised to send to me by runner. The women told me that the only men they wanted around them on the mountain were Sherpa high-altitude porters. They had to accept that no expedition could manage to carry equipment and supplies to high camps on the mountain without these men. They

3

told me that people would say they had had help from a man if I was present in the area!

The *Daily Express* was then the leading Fleet Street broadsheet newspaper selling over four-and-a-quarter million copies a day, boasting that its reports came from 'Expressmen on the spot'. Its great editor Arthur Christiansen became ill and was replaced by Edward Pickering. When I told him about the women's attitude over a male reporter covering the expedition from on the spot, he told me he was sure I would manage to overcome the ladies' objections.

'What, no cleft sticks, old man?' scoffed my colleagues as 3 cwt of camping gear and supplies (including packs of army compo rations sufficient for 56 days and 22 pounds of service biscuits kindly sold to me by the War Office) piled up in the office. At a Piccadilly store I bought G.B. Shaw-type knickerbockers, a wool-lined windproof nylon anorak, a balaclava, leather gloves with silk under-gloves, woollen stockings, fine light Italian climbing boots, crampons, a ridge tent, sleeping bag, air mattress, rucksack and oil compass. A surgical instrument shop supplied the contents of a first aid box to cover possible accidents and to dispense medicine to ailing people along the way, expected of a travelling Sahib. I bought malaria and stomach pills and various other things which an Indian shop assistant told me I would not be able to find in New Delhi. One was foot-ointment, for he explained that in the subcontinent 'the poor have hardened feet and the rich don't walk'. That was the best advice I was given, and I emptied two jars into an aluminium container.

My picture, dressed in mountain gear surrounded by my equipment and stores was published across six columns the day before I flew in a Comet airliner towards this fabulous opportunity for adventure. My heavy gear was aboard the steamship Johannesburg bound from Liverpool to Calcutta for onward delivery to me at the Royal Hotel, Kathmandu.

Chapter Two

Leader's Obsession with Cho Oyu, the Difficult Mountain

An elfin figure, 4 foot 10 inches tall, attractive with fair hair and grey-blue eyes, held the admiring attention of 50 members of the Ladies Alpine Club, a gathering of Britain's top women mountain climbers. The speaker, Madame Claude Kogan of Nice, had stood on the summits of all the great classic climbs in the French, Swiss and Italian Alps, and had sought higher challenge in the Andes before taking on one of the Himalayan giants. In 1953 with a male companion, Pierre Vilfor, she had made the first ascent of Nun Kun (7,135 metres, 23,410 feet) in Kashmir on which British attempts had failed in 1934 and 1946. That gave her the women's high-altitude record. She improved on it in 1954 when she climbed to a height of 7,700 metres (25,496 feet), achieved on a Himalayan peak called Cho Oyu. She had climbed not only higher than any other woman, but also higher than all but a handful of men.

Her talk to this group of British women was mainly about that climb on Cho Oyu. Claude Kogan had achieved that record altitude as a member of a small Swiss expedition led by the renowned climber Raymond Lambert. They had made the three-week-long trek across Nepal to Cho Oyu only to find that an Austrian expedition was already on the mountain. They had to wait while the Austrians made their summit attempts; the first failed but in a second attempt on October 19th they succeeded. The leader, Herbert Tichy, who later suffered severe frostbite, S. Jochler and Sherpa Pasang and Dama Lama were the first to stand on the summit of Cho Oyu.

Meanwhile, two male members of the four-strong Swiss expedition suffered altitude sickness so badly that they had to be escorted down the mountain by the party's only two Sherpas, leaving Lambert and Kogan alone in an ice cave at their Camp Four. On October 20th the summit was clear and Raymond Lambert and Claude Kogan were able to continue their climb. They left the ice

5

cave at 9 a.m. roped together, wearing crampons, confident of scaling the final 2,900 feet of the mountain, despite a strong wind blowing. Soon the wind grew stronger, forcing them to climb one at a time, both falling flat when the worst gusts came. They crawled up snow slopes on all fours, running out 60 feet of rope at a time.

This is how Madame Kogan described the experience in *White Fury*, the book about the expedition she co-authored with Raymond Lambert. 'I had never had such a furious struggle with the elements. At every gust we shut our eyes tightly and the whipped-up snow lacerated our skin, its frozen dust stifling us and penetrating every chink in our clothing. But we went on, bent double, step by step, willing ourselves onward.

'Once more Raymond stopped to refasten his crampon. And this time he looked at his watch and the altimeter. I knew what he was going to say and I dared not look at him. We had reached 25,600 feet (7,800 metres).' It was 2 p.m. and it would have taken them at least three more hours to reach the summit. Lambert decided that they had to turn back. Claude Kogan argued that they still had time to reach the summit, but Lambert remained firm.

She wrote, 'I felt myself boiling with impotent rage, ready to dare anything if we could continue with the struggle. Although my reason saw the only logical decision to take, my heart refused to accept it.

'I didn't wish to bow my head before the wind and snow that must eventually hurl us back. "Don't turn back yet", I gasped. "It's no use Claude", Lambert said, "There's nothing for it. we'll have to go down." For a moment we stayed motionless as though refusing to let go before starting down. Indeed that moment, when we had to turn our backs on the objective for which we had sacrificed so much and for so long, was a terrible one.'

She did, however, have the consolation of gaining a new women's altitude record, having reached 25,496 feet.

That male decision, baulking Madame Kogan's ambition to reach the summit of Cho Oyu, was the catalyst for the idea of an exclusively female expedition, and also the reason why their target was the summit of Cho Oyu, known as a difficult climb. Only a year before the successful British 1953 Everest expedition, famed mountaineer Eric Shipton had led a training party to Cho Oyu, including Edmund Hilary and Sherpa Tenzing, who would be the first to stand on the summit of the world's highest. The expedition was to try out young British climbers, study monsoon conditions and test oxygen equipment in preparation for the full-scale attempt on Everest. They got nowhere near the summit of Cho Oyu. Bad weather forced them to turn back as they reached the foot of a 250-foot ice cliff at 22,000 feet.

Madame Kogan rounded off her talk at the Ladies Alpine Club by saying 'The Alps must not remain the only objective of women's expeditions. They are just a springboard. Our goal, from now on, is the Himalayas.' She added wistfully, 'If only this summit [Cho Oyu] could be the first to be climbed by women!'

This tiny Parisian woman had begun climbing as a teenager named Claude Trouillet in the Belgian Ardennes just before the war. During the German occupation she joined her mother who had taken refuge at Nice, journeying without papers through forested ridges to avoid German checkpoints on the demarcation line with Vichy territory. From her new home in Nice she began climbing the Alps on Sundays with local mountaineers, some of whom laughed at the mountaineering ambitions expressed by such a slight, frail-looking woman.

One Sunday she took a bus to Saint-Jeannet, and climbed alone towards the summit of a minor peak called Le Baou. When she reached the top she found a dark-haired youth there eating a snack. He was Georges Kogan, of Russian origin, who made the mountains a refuge from the Gestapo. Claude took Georges food from the family rations every weekend until the time she found the old chalet where he lived deserted. Georges had been captured, but the Allied landings in Normandy saved him from deportation, and he was reunited with Claude in November 1944. They married in 1945.

Georges owned a knitwear business, and Claude, a top seamstress in a fashion house, joined him in designing and manufacturing swimsuits under the brand name of 'Fontaine'. The business prospered well, financing their climbing holidays.

When they had climbed most Alpine peaks together the Kogans decided to make their first overseas expedition to the Andes. In 1951 they climbed the Cordillera Blanc in the Andes with Alpinist friends, and with one of them, Nicole Leininger, Madame Kogan climbed Quitarajo (6,120 metres, 20,276 feet). This was the first time women had climbed on their own to such an altitude.

Six months after that Georges Kogan became ill and died.

Madame Kogan, always wearing a silver necklace containing a smiling picture of her late husband, sought consolation in climbing higher and higher. On each summit she left a silver brooch containing a picture of her late husband. She returned to the Andes in 1952, leading a party to the summit of Salcantay (20,574 feet), and made her first climb in the Himalayas a year later. During this 1953 climb with male companion, Pierre Vittoz, she made the first ascent of Nun Kun (7,135 metres, 23,410 feet) in Kashmir.

With another Swiss expedition in 1955, Madame Kogan made another first ascent, reaching the 24,298-foot peak of Ganesh in western Nepal with Raymond Lambert and E. Gauchat. Madame Kogan went to Greenland in 1956, and in 1957 she returned to the Andes with Raymond Lambert and the Belgian Alpinist Claudine van der Stratten to climb Cayesh (18.769 feet). In 1958 she climbed Elbruz (18,481 feet) in the Caucasus, the highest peak in Europe.

I met Madame Kogan for the first time in the summer of 1959, a month before the all-woman expedition began. I entertained .her and two English members of the expedition, Countess Dorothea Gravina, wife of an Italian nobleman, and Miss Margaret Darvall, head of a secretarial college in Hampstead, to dinner in the Hotel Negresco on the Riviera shore.

I was surprised to find Claude Kogan so petite, but quickly discovered that her lack of stature was countered by iron determination. Firmly, she refused to comment on whether Raymond Lambert's decision to turn back on Cho Oyu, when the summit was so near, was the reason for her organising an all-woman expedition in which as leader she would make all key decisions.

At the time I noted, 'I have rarely met anyone so determined. What she wants she really goes after, I would think, with ruthless disregard of everything else. I asked her why she felt impelled to pit her feminine strength against piercing winds, thin air, ice hazards and all the other dangers of trying to conquer one of the sister peaks of Everest. She answered simply "Because I like it."'

There was no psychological talk of fulfilment, nothing about years of perhaps being called a 'Tich' and wanting to show the world that, petite as she was, she could conquer the tallest mountains. She had, after all, already climbed higher among the silent grandeur of the Himalayan peaks than any other woman and all but a handful of men. It had recently been reported from China that eight Chinese women who had reached the summit of 24,750-

foot Mustagh Ata in the Pamirs, were claiming to share among them the credit for breaking a women's altitude record set up by Madame Claude Kogan in 1955.

Madame Kogan was dismissive, pointing out that the Chinese women had been in an expedition with 25 men, and all 33 climbers were said to have reached the summit. She said, 'I still hold the women's altitude record for my climb on Cho Oyu in 1954. The reference to 1955 was when I reached the summit of Ganesh Himal (24,298 feet). So it is true that the Chinese women have established a new summit height record.' She was clearly in no doubt that she would soon regain the summit record by climbing all the way up Cho Oyu.

Asked what was the advantage of having no men in her party, she replied, 'Without men about I am sure women can work together as a team in the same way as men can without women. That way the important thing, the only thing, will be the mountain. Petty jealousies will not arise.'

But she showed the typical feminine coyness of that time when asked about the women's ages, replying 'You can say we average 30.' She gave me a Sphinx-like smile when I asked whether there might be an all-female attempt on Everest if they succeeded on Cho Oyu. 'Maybe,' she replied.

Together we caught the Mistral Express to Marseilles next day where two of the English climbers were to accompany the expedition's 4 tons of gear and stores in the liner *Laos* bound for Calcutta, the nearest port to the Himalayas.

I had first met Miss Darvall, 37, several weeks earlier in her drawing room at the secretarial college in Hampstead. The girls learning shorthand and typing in the rooms around us, and Miss Darvall in a summer dress among the chintz chair covers, had seemed a far cry from the high snow peaks we had talked about. She told me she had climbed the major Alpine peaks and looked for new targets in the Himalayas. She added, 'I climb mountains because it is so different from my ordinary life. It's an escape for me.'

Countess Gravina had been absent when I had called at her aptly named Rose Cottage near the Kent village of Frittenden on a fine summer's day two weeks before. She had been in hospital for an appendicitis operation and the sea voyage to India was to be her convalescence. The former Miss Dorothea Briggs from Yorkshire had married the Italian Count Gravina, a musician and conductor, in 1934. When war broke out she took their two sons to America where she gave birth to a third son. Her husband was killed in the Italian army in North Africa. She had climbed 18,500-foot Kilimanjaro in her twenties, lived in the Italian Tyrol from 1934 to 1939, and at the age of 53 had joined a rock-climbing course for beginners in Skye. She was clearly the oldest of the Cho Oyu party, grey-haired, her face set in an almost permanent smile, and tanned by many hours in her garden that fine English summer.

During the train journey Madame Kogan expressed worry about my being assigned to cover their expedition, and despite the £2,000 the *Daily Express* contributed towards it, paid under a contract promising that all expedition members would give the *Express* exclusive co-operation in covering the story, she made it clear that she expected me to report from Kathmandu, relying on messages they sent to me by runner.

Miss Darvall, who began serious climbing in 1955 and was regarded by fellow Alpinists as an 'efficient if not brilliant rock climber', agreed. She said, 'We don't want a man anywhere near us because people will only belittle our achievement by saying there was a man standing by in case we got into trouble.'

I refrained from mentioning that they would be relying on an all-male team of Sherpas to carry their tents and supplies up the mountain slopes, but did make it clear that my office would expect me to report from the mountain.

Every ship in Marseilles harbour was dressed in bunting, not to mark the departure of the women climbers, but for a double national celebration. It was Bastille Day and Liberation Day.

On the Sunday before the third British member of the expedition, Mrs Eileen Healey, left home to fly to Nepal, I met her and her husband in a top floor flat in Tonbridge, Kent. Pictures of high snow peaks were around the walls, and bookshelves were crammed with mountain literature. The couple had met on the summit of the Black Rocks in Derbyshire, and their first wedding anniversary coincided with her departure for Paris to link up with the continental climbers and accompany them on their flight to New Delhi.

Mr Dick Healey, 31-year-old chemistry master at Tonbridge School, told me, 'Eileen would have liked to back out because it meant we would miss spending our first anniversary together, but I could not allow her to miss a wonderful opportunity like this.' Mrs

Healey, 32, better known at that time as Eileen Gregory, her maiden name, was president of the Pinnacle Club, the British rock climbers' association. Although the youngest of the British trio she was the only one of them with experience beyond the Alps, having made the first summit climb of Cathedral Peak in the Indian Punjab with women companions in 1956.

Madame Kogan and six other expedition members were staying in an inexpensive hotel behind Connaught Circus in New Delhi, and on my arrival I invited them to dine with me. Heads turned when the seven women arrived at the restaurant of the newly opened Ashoka Hotel where I was staying. The most striking of them was glamorous Claudine van der Stratten, a Belgian aristocrat and former companion of Princess Charlotte, on leave from a job in a Paris fashion salon. She had blonde-flecked hair, blue eyes, a mannequin stance, and looked as though she had stepped from a model parade. She wore figure-clinging slacks and a bright bush shirt blouse with a golfing motif. Her toe and finger nails were manicured and varnished. She was a girl to look at more than twice anywhere. When we talked in their New Delhi hotel she bemoaned the loss of some of her beauty aids which Madame Kogan had thrown out of her case before leaving Paris. She lamented 'All she left me was the red nail varnish because she said that might be useful in marking numbers of loads.'

The others were Madame Jeanne Franco, 40, the copper-haired wife of an instructor at the Chamonix school of mountaineering, who told me, 'I began climbing only after my marriage 20 years ago. I climbed because my husband did. Now I must go on to higher and higher peaks.' Loulou Boulaz, 34, had climbed every difficult rock face and route in the Alps in her spare time from being a verbatim shorthand writer with the International Labour Office. She said, 'I like the excitement that the dangers of climbing provide.' Michelin Ramboud, was an official photographer working for *Paris-Match*. Dr Colette le Bret, 35, a village doctor from near Nantes, began climbing when she became doctor to a climbing school. She said, 'I caught the bug.'

The seven expedition women and I left Delhi together aboard a dawn Indian Airlines Dakota for Patna, where we had to land for passport and customs checks before getting back on the same plane to fly on to Kathmandu. There had been a one-day pilots' strike the day before, causing a backlog of passengers, and the pilot was not one of those who flew regularly into Kathmandu. We took off from Patna in clear weather as we crossed the jungle-covered Terai foothills, but cloud hid the peaks on either side of the Chandragiri Pass that were higher than the Dakota's cruising height. Half an hour after take-off the pilot announced we were turning back to Patna. I thought he was a bit faint-hearted.

We lunched on fried eggs, toast and beer at Patna's poky airport building, and just as the weather cleared our plane was ordered back to Delhi to meet another schedule. I was furious. From my previous visit three years before, I knew that the normal connection for Kathmandu started from Calcutta, and passengers from Delhi transferred to it in Patna. The plane from Calcutta had taken off just as we returned to Patna and made it into Kathmandu. So did a plane on charter to the United States Embassy.

There was every prospect of a long delay because Indian Airlines gave priority to passengers already booked leaving stranded passengers to wait for spare seats. Among those delayed with us was Boris Lissanevitch, the White Russian proprietor of the Royal Hotel in Kathmandu, his lovely Danish wife Inga (who both figure in Han Suyin's novel *The Mountain is Young*) and their three small sons. Boris, whom I knew from my stay in the Royal Hotel during my previous sojourn in Nepal, told me he was taking the Ganges ferry, an overnight train and the rugged road over 8,000-foot passes rather than depend on the vagaries of Indian Airlines. Before this road, built by Indian army engineers, opened a short time before, Kathmandu had been one of the world's most inaccessible capitals, four days by mule from Patna.

On hearing that landslides had caused delays on the road into Nepal I decided to take my chance on the next plane, and advised the women climbers to do likewise. An airline bus took us into Patna, capital of the desperately poor Bihar state, unprepossessing in the dingy, overcrowded, junkyard way of provincial India. I expected the hotel to be dreadful, and was pleasantly surprised to find the Republican Hotel offered splendid service. Despite its position above a transport showroom on a dirt street crowded with bicycle rickshaws, the combined dining room-lounge was well furnished and air conditioned.

The ladies were by this time pulling my leg a lot, and there was rapid banter in French about which one of them should room with me! I had a room with a bath, but the bearer had forgotten a

12

mosquito net and I was badly bitten during a long sleepless night of torture. However, there was no Prohibition (which did exist in most Indian states) and we had a jolly, friendly dinner, stormbound at 190 feet above sea level. It was not until I saw the bill that I discovered that Bihar charges a prohibitive tax for being a 'wet state', making whisky the equivalent of 10s 6d a shot.

There was chaos at the airport next day, and in the mêlée I managed to get a seat. So did Madame Kogan and two others of her team. One of those left behind until next day's flight was Claudine. My diary note reads, 'She put on all her charm and told me it was important for them to get to Kathmandu, and she would be obliged if I would let her have my seat. I told her it was important for me, too, as the only representative of my paper.' The pilot, a regular on the route, flew across the Chandragiri Pass between peaks hidden by cloud, descended into Kathmandu Valley, lying at 4,000 feet, and made a sharp spiral with the starboard wingtip seeming almost to touch a cliff face, to land on a 1,200-yard-long strip between a precipice and three deep gorges.

A large crowd welcomed the climbers. Tenzing of Everest was at the bottom of the aircraft steps, wearing flannels and a blazer with the white peak badge of his Darjeeling mountaineering school on the pocket. With him were his two daughters, pretty 18-year-old Pem-Pem and plumpish 17-year-old Nima, and his 24-year-old niece, Duma, all in bright saris. Beside them were Countess Gravina and Margaret Darvall, deeply suntanned since we had last met in Marseilles. Lined up on the edge of the tarmac were eleven stocky high-altitude Sherpas, men without whom climbers in the Himalayas, whether men or women, stood no chance of success.

The expedition women were driven along a narrow newly completed road in Landrovers to the edge of a city of golden-roofed pagodas to stay at the rambling Royal Hotel, once a palace belonging to the Rana family. Successive heads of this family had ruled Nepal as hereditary Prime Ministers for more than a century until a palace coup a few years earlier had freed the monarch from virtual house arrest. It was the Ranas who kept Nepal a land forbidden to foreigners, except for an Embassy which the British rulers of neighbouring India had insisted on having there.

The two advance-party women and Tenzing had preparations well advanced. A huge pile of expedition stores and equipment was stowed in a lock-up hut in the grounds of the Indian Embassy, and

13

Countess Gravina and Miss Darvall were staying in a tent in the grounds to keep an eye on it. The Tenzing girls, on special leave from their convent school in Darjeeling, were staying more comfortably as guests of the Indian Ambassador. After India's independence, the large Embassy and Residence owned by Britain was handed over as the Indian Embassy, while a small modern building further down the road housed the more modest present British Embassy.

Because Margaret Darvall was coughing badly, Eileen Healey took her place in the tent and Darvall was ordered to stay in bed at the Royal Hotel. She got up the day before the expedition departed.

Clothing was issued to the eleven high-altitude Sherpas, red woollen ski-type caps that pulled down over face and ears, exactly like the ones the women were to wear, and white-striped blue woollen shirts. By the time they joined the queue for windproof clothing most of them had already changed into the stylish new rigs. The women's trekking uniform, gifts from a Paris fashion house, was figure-clinging sky-blue slacks and pink sweaters. But the muscular Eileen Healey couldn't get into hers and had to go to the hotel tailor to adapt them to her figure.

Claudine van der Stratten arrived the following day with the other three stragglers. She was wearing leggings of mottled gold material with a short-sleeved blouse to match. At a party in the British Embassy she wore an elegant cocktail dress, looking as though she had stepped from the cover of a fashion magazine. She confided in me that she was already finding Himalayan climbing disturbingly different from her Alpine experience. She said, 'I dread the thought of the approach march, and having nobody but women for company for the next three months.'

I said that most of her companions seemed happy to be getting away from men and civilisation, happy that without men they would have all responsibility themselves. Claudine gave me a mischievous wink, saying, 'For me, having no men has no advantage. I don't like responsibility anyway.'

Just why did she want to climb Cho Oyu, then?

'To me climbing is a sport like any other. When you have climbed everything in the Alps you must come to the Himalayas to find a new challenge. Just like at golf you keep on trying to be a scratch player. But I don't like the long exile from normal life that climbing here entails.'

14

Countess Gravina was doing most of the donkey work, rising from her tent sleeping bag at dawn to apportion the 40 tons of gear and supplies into 60-pound carrying loads, joined by those in the hotel only at 10 a.m. The job of unpacking, repacking and weighing on hanging scales had been handicapped most of the time by drenching rain. At the last minute the British women were embarrassed to find that all their foreign companions had brought small versions of their national flags with them. The flags of France, Belgium, Switzerland, Nepal and India were to be tied to an ice axe and planted on the summit of Cho Oyu. They appealed to the British Embassy, but the only flag of suitable size was the one the Ambassador flew on his car, and that carried a special crest. The best that could be done was to have a copy made in the bazaar,[1] a most rudimentary effort.

How did they make such an omission in 4 tons of gear, escorted from Europe to Nepal by two British women? Countess Gravina said, 'We just never thought about it. But as everybody else has brought a flag along we don't want to be left out.'

The woman were aware that I was intent on following them to Cho Oyu, as I made no secret of that. Countess Gravina tried to assure me that they would send me full details of their progress as fast as they could. She added smugly, 'Madame Kogan and I have seen the Prime Minister. We have no problem with you or any other newspaperman visiting the mountain. You will be refused permission to visit the area on grounds of the critical frontier situation.'

When all the gear was sorted and ready for the porters there was more delay because the banks were closed for two days of public holiday. The expedition needed sack-loads of small-denomination money to pay porters and buy fresh food along the along the route. Tenzing was clearly harassed by frequent palavers over organisation, but maintained his good humour. He told me that he thought the expedition might be on the mountain before the monsoon ended, and explained, 'They might find much snow still on the

---

[1] The *Daily Express* bought a flag, cabling to say it was on its way by Comet to Calcutta, but it never appeared aboard the daily Indian Airline planes arriving from Calcutta. Eventually I found it held by Indian customs despite being consigned to Nepal, only in transit through India. Later it took me three days of cajoling at Calcutta customs, where the need for an import licence was waived on payment of 9 rupees (about 13s 6d) duty. The clearing agent cost another 16 rupees (24s.) and after all that the flag was too big, 43 inches by 23! Anyone trying to hold it on top of Cho Oyu would have been blown off!

mountain, very tiring to climb through, also dangerous from avalanches if the weather suddenly got warmer. It needs time for the snow to settle and leave a fine firm surface for crampons.'

Another time he said, 'One of these days, I suppose, they will be trying Everest', adding almost prophetically, 'But they will find Cho Oyu[2] tough going. It is a very windy mountain, and has a bad reputation for storms with winds of more than 80 miles an hour.'

On the eve of the expedition's departure from Kathmandu, Countess Gravina asked me to escort her and Eileen Healey back to their camp as extra security for a money-bag full of cash just obtained from the bank. I was surprised at this uncharacteristic recourse to the aid of a man, though, of course, they relied heavily on Sherpa men. It was a beautiful moonlit night as we strolled the mile to the Indian Embassy, and we were quite merry from repeated champagne toasts to the expedition's success at a farewell party given by Boris Lissanevitch and his wife.

Countess Gravina, who at that time had no ambition to make the summit herself, told me, 'I am going to bag a 20,000-foot peak that has never been climbed as a training climb. It's actually over the border in Tibet, but keep that under your hat. I do want to be first to tread the summit of a peak before I die.'

Eileen Healey, who had already achieved that, expressed surprise. 'I don't see that it makes any difference. It's the climb I enjoy, not the thought that nobody has been there before.' She also expressed her own doubts about the choice of Cho Oyu. She felt that the 22,000-foot barrier – the stage at which rarefied air makes breathing extremely difficult and can effect judgement – might defeat all those without previous high-altitude experience. That meant all of them except Madame Kogan, who had decided that oxygen would not be used. The six oxygen cyclinders in the expedition equipment were for medicinal use only, in case of pneumonia – one more of the deadly hazards of Himalayan climbing. This comment confirmed what I had been suspecting for some time. The expedition was conceived and organised with one major objective – to put Madame Claude Kogan on top of a mountain that had beaten her when her companion was a man.

---

[2] The summit of Cho Oyu had been climbed for a second time just a year before – by an Indian expedition whose leader died of pneumonia at Base Camp.

Chapter Three

Setting Out for Namche Bazar

To reach the mountain from Kathmandu the women had to travel on foot for over three weeks, a trek of some 200 miles over 17 passes, some over 15,000 feet high, descending to jungle valleys as low as 3,000 feet, crossing frothing rivers by tree-trunk bridges or swaying catwalks – entering a lost world of medieval monasteries and temples where man was himself the beast of burden, and where, in an age of moon rockets, there were no wheeled vehicles of any kind. The only wheels were used to swing prayers around instead of reciting them.

At first light on Friday, August 21st, Countess Gravina and Eileen Healey, sheltering from drenching rain under a chic red umbrella, began checking out loads to be carried to the mountain by 164 porters, 40 of them women. As each porter collected a load from the pile in the corrugated iron shed, he or she was handed a numbered card which was entered against their name in the load book. Male porters were at the head of the queue to pick up the loads, carrying them in turn to the shelter of a porch at the entrance to the Indian Ambassador's residence, where they smoked a cigarette while making their loads more comfortable to carry with bits of rope and sacking they had brought with them. When the last porters had taken their loads and joined the long, straggling line of porters, the women returned to the hotel for a leisurely breakfast.

The rain stopped as they were ready to leave, and in bright sunshine they were driven in two Landrovers, jolting and bumping along a mud track towards the distant peaks through a terrain of steaming paddy fields, waving at their burdened porters as they overtook them.

At the exotic temple town of Bhadgoan, 7 miles from Kathmandu, the Landrovers paused for the women to enjoy tourism, ranging around temples and idols with cameras clicking. Back on the trail the track became rocky and one of the Landrovers had a puncture. As its passengers sat on a bank beside the track watching the wheel being changed, a Nepalese lady passed

17

snootily by in a travel chair carried by two muscular men. A tinker also appeared and sold Countess Gravina a souvenir, a tiny butter lamp for about a farthing.

The Landrovers pressed on up steep bends with sharp drops on one side to the top of Chowki Pass. There the track ended, just 11 miles from the capital. Beyond that no wheeled traffic was thought to go at that time. Some of the women found this short drive rather frightening. Loulou Boulaz, a star Alpine climber from Geneva, commented, 'I've experienced nothing like it. I'd rather walk.'

The vehicles parked in the tiny square of a village at the top of the pass and the women ate a picnic lunch under the astonished gaze of the few inhabitants and the lenses of newsreel cameras. The press were the Kathmandu correspondents of Indian newspapers, most of them also acting as stringers (locally employed correspondents) for London newspapers.

Rain began again as the women said goodbye to a small group of people who had driven to the end of the road to see them off. Madame Kogan smiled, 'It is lucky for expeditions to start out in the rain.'

The women were dressed in their colourful trekking gear – all except Claudine van der Stratten, an individualist who wore her gold leggings with matching blouse, contrasting with the sombre black of a locally bought umbrella. As the rain came on harder the women put on red plastic capes.

Eileen Healey, happy to be setting out for the mountains, led the procession at a brisk pace in company with Margaret Darvall, still suffering occasional coughing bouts but looking fit and cheerful. The others paired off too, but Claudine strode along alone looking purposeful. Madame Kogan, much more relaxed than she had been for days, brought up the rear with Countess Gravina, laughing and joking happily together. The local reporters and newsreel cameramen turned back after a few hundred yards.

The shower soon passed and the women trekked on in sunshine through terraced paddy fields of vivid green against a background of jungle-clad hills. Country people gazed in amazement at this parade of Memsahibs. Along the way they met a man with a baby in one of two baskets balanced across his shoulders. The babe's weight was counterbalanced by goods in the other basket. Some of these remarkable women paused to chuck the infant under its chin.

After five miles the women filed through the market town of

Banepa, where commerce in the market place came to a stop as the women paraded through it. From the town's single track the climbers could see the last porters, who had begun their 16-mile march ten hours before, climbing a steep hill beyond the town. There on a small grass plateau the Sherpas had already pitched camp for the first night stop. Brightly coloured camp tables and chairs were set out, and two chickens and a pan of rice were already cooking on a camp fire.

As the only member of the press to follow the women to their first night camp, I used the last of my film, swigged a drop of cold tea from Eileen Healey's flask, bid the ladies goodbye and good luck, and hurried back alone along the way they had marched.

On the way I met Sherpa Tenzing and his three girls, who had started out later than the rest of the party, and cursed my luck at not having one shot left in either of my two cameras (one for colour, one for black and white). When I reached the village at the top of Chowki Pass every vehicle, including the Landrover I had hired, had left. My rivals had nobbled my transport in order to make me late filing. After trotting down the twisting track for four weary miles to Bhadgoan, the only wheeled vehicle I met was a bicycle ridden by a boy, but I could not make him understand my offer of 20 rupees to allow me to ride pillion to Bhadgoan. It was dusk when I passed through the temple squares of Bhadgoan, bustling with praying crowds and masked dancers.

On our way out that morning I had noticed buses parked on the Kathmandu side of town, and they were still there but I could find no drivers. I pressed on wearily and at the end of a long straight stretch of road saw a jeep at the roadside with its bonnet up. Just as I got to it the engine burst into life, and although there were nine passengers already they squeezed up and made room for me. The journey was still agonisingly slow, with the driver cruising downhill to save petrol, and stalling twice on steep gradients.

At the hotel I swallowed a large Scotch, grabbed my typewriter and had the luxury of a Landrover to myself to go to the cable office, where the Indian staff allowed me to use a table in their office and despatched my cables take by take as I dashed them off.

Next evening, still sore and stiff, I had a long talk with Tenzing, back from spending the night in Banepa and seeing the women off on their second day's trek. He told me that torrential rain had fallen all night.

19

He added, 'They set off early this morning in high spirits despite the downpour. The only worry was for Miss Darvall because she was coughing badly. They had breakfast at 5.30 a.m., fried eggs and fried chapatti bread with a choice of coffee or tea.' He was clearly thrilled that his daughter Pem-Pem was a sharing a tent with Mademoiselle Claudine.

Tenzing told me that he was born in Tami, a village two days' walk from the Khumbu glacier, and that his parents and sisters still lived there. He had begun as a porter in 1933 when Shipton described him in his account of the Everest expedition as 'young, keen, strong and very likeable'. He reached 27,560 feet on Everest as Sirdar with the Swiss expedition in 1952, and had joined the British 1953 expedition for 300 rupees (£20) a month. He told me that Sherpas found British expeditions much less generous than the Swiss and others, and often British climbers treated them shabbily.

Tenzing stayed on several more days in Kathmandu delayed by a trade union problem. He had asked to see the Prime Minister to appeal against a threat to ruin his Darjeeling-based business providing Sherpas and porters to expeditions. He had handled the hiring of the Sherpas and porters for the women's expedition, and most of the jobs went to people whose names were on the books of his Darjeeling Association, patronised by his fellow Everesters, Sir John Hunt and Sir Edmund Hilary. It was both benevolent organisation and employment bureau. Several of the women's high-altitude Sherpas were instructors at the Indian Climbing Institute where he was chief instructor. There was much resentment among local Sherpas and porters at expedition jobs being monopolised by Tenzing's mountaineering elite. Just a year before, a Himalayan Society had been founded to represent their interests. Its President was Ang Babu, a plump man with a gold-toothed smile, who was also a member of the Upper House of the Nepalese Parliament.

Through him, a new law had now been added to an already formidable list of expedition rules, making it compulsory for future expeditions to employ Sherpas and porters through the society, thus shutting out Tenzing's association. When Tenzing saw the newly elected Prime Minister Koirala a few days later, he obtained a promise that if Tenzing opened a branch of his agency in Kathmandu with Sherpas and porters resident in Nepal on his books he would be given equal recognition with the Himalayan Society.

Travel outside the immediate Kathmandu area was prohibited for foreigners without a special travel permit, so my first task after the women's departure was to obtain a permit to visit the Namche Bazar area. I found the office of the Foreign Secretary, a permanent official, in the palatial rambling warren called the Singha Durbar where all government offices and activities from state banquets to storage of archives were held. He spoke of political difficulties about allowing foreigners to travel in frontier areas, and it looked as though the ladies might succeed in confining me to Kathmandu.

I asked to see the Prime Minister, Bisweswar Prasad Koirala (his name means 'By God's mercy master of the world'). He had swept to power a few months earlier when his Nepali Congress Party won 74 of the 109 parliamentary seats. I talked with the Prime Minister in his office in the Singha Durbar, He was a studious-looking man of 43, quiet-spoken in the flawless English he had learned at Calcutta University. He was dressed in white jodhpurs, a cotton shirt buttoned over in Cossack style, a coloured high-crowned skullcap, and a pin-striped Western-style jacket. First we talked of Nepal's problems, of development and the dangers of envelopment from north and south.

Then I presented my petition stating what I wanted to do, asking for permission to travel to the Namche Bazar region. In my presence the Prime Minister rang the Foreign Secretary to tell him he approved my petition. But anxious weeks passed before I could get it in writing.

At dawn every morning I took long training walks, and learned all I could about a land still little known beyond the surrounding mountains. Often men I passed in the streets peeled off a smart salute, revealing themselves as Gurkha pensioners. The hotel *chowkidar* (watchman), a little Ghurkha with two rows of British campaign ribbons, always snapped to attention and saluted when I passed.

One of my walks was to a great stupa at Bodnath several miles north of the city, where I met the Tibetan abbot known as the Chini Lama. The temple has large painted eyes looking out on all sides. I also went again to the Hanuman Dhoka, the temple of the monkey god whose pillars are surmounted by lascivious stone carvings. I had watched the King's coronation there three summers before.

21

Colonel Jimmy Roberts, Military Attaché at the British Embassy, gave me much useful advice, and we had many meals together. He was an ex-Gurkha officer, and had been transport officer with the 1953 Everest expedition. He agreed to receive my runners, pay them on a scale that they could increase for each day they were swifter than the traditional *dak* (postal) runners' average of eight days from Namche Bazar, and send my messages from the cable office just across the road from the Embassy.[1]

A 25-year-old descendant of the Ranas, Uttram Shumshere, who had just been appointed Under-Secretary at the Home Office in charge of press and broadcasting, became a good chum. He had lived abroad for six years, having spent two years at Clacton Tech, two years at the London School of Journalism, and two years as a reporter on the *Kensington News*. He dined with me at the Royal Hotel where life-sized portraits of his ancestors hung around the walls, and he told me the story of each of them. Behind his chair was a painting of his great-grandfather, resplendent in scarlet and gold, feather and noble order, who had murdered an uncle to take power. Mostly he liked to talk about his job, and sounded me out on his idea to link a country cut off by lack of roads and transport with a 'Down Your Way' radio programme, a snag being that the presenter would have to trek for weeks and send tape recordings back by runner. At the next table another evening were five genial Russian airmen, come from Moscow to fly King Mahendra on a tour of India in their Ilyushin plane.

One evening we attended a production of Western drama in the dancing room of an old Rana palace with Her Brittanic Majesty's Ambassador, Leonard Scopes, as one of the star actors. The Hams, Himalayan Amateurs, performed *The Man Who Came to Dinner*. The top people attended, the King and Queen and all the princes and princesses, the army command, the entire diplomatic community. A princess presented all the cast with a bouquet at the final curtain. It played to packed audiences for three more nights – a pleasant interlude amid worries over delays in being able to follow the women to the mountains.

Eight days passed before two pigtailed runners brought back the first messages about the expedition's progress along the arduous

---

[1] Colonel Roberts later went into business organising trekking holidays.

trail to the high peaks pioneered by previous post-war expeditions. They had taken two days from the women's fifth overnight camp.

In a long note to me dated August 26th, Countess Gravina noted the place as Kirantichap ('and if you can find that on the map its more than I can') apologising for not having time to put pen to paper before this.

She explained, 'I have charge of all the equipment, and with 180 loads coming into camp, many long after dark, and all sorts of things having to be found in all sorts of odd boxes or bags, you can imagine each evening has been pretty fully occupied. Then some nights it has rained tigers and elephants, you know just how it can, and everything has to be piled up, covered with tarpaulins and trenches dug around to keep things from floating away altogether. The most useful things to keep loads dry are little Nepalese roofs made of cane with leaves laid in between; all our Nepalese porters have them to walk along with over their heads and everything keeps wonderful dry.

'After leaving you we walked round and round hills and through miles of wet paddy fields. The people we meet are friendly and kind everywhere we go. Of course, the interest and curiosity is enormous. They have never in their lives seen 12 Memsahibs on the march! High up above it we came upon a river, and suddenly saw a bridge at the end of the day's march. Two of us nipped up a nice little stream and found the ideal spot, a pool to wash in and a higher pool to rinse in and a waterfall to get under – after a long hot day it was bliss. Then over a long suspension bridge across a wide swift-flowing river, up to a rocky knoll and below on the other side was another great river.

'There was a small rest-house perched on the knoll above the village of Dolalghat. It had a mud-floored veranda below, a room above with open windows all round, no glass, just big gaps. Soon the porters began to come in and dumped their loads in great piles; the upper room looked like a crowded school dormitory with our twelve camp beds crammed into it.

'Down below was a seething mass of porters making their little cooking fires. Our cooking and eating place was a little further along the ridge, among the rocks where the Sherpas camped. The doctor opened up her enormous first aid case and soon the usual evening surgery began, not only for our porters but for people from the village as well – mostly blisters and infected sores, eye troubles and anything from aches in the legs to a tired heart. The best one can do in such cases is a pill of some sort, the brighter coloured the better.

'These people have no medical aid anywhere within reach and so have developed pretty healthy powers of healing and resistance to infections, otherwise they would all be dead. We can help a lot with disinfecting sores and cuts on feet so that they heal quickly.

'On Sunday, August 23rd the Sherpas appeared at 5 a.m. with bowls of tea. Complete confusion in our dormitory with all of us trying to dress and pack bags and rucksacks at the same moment and Sherpas trying to fold up lightweight beds and get our kitbags to make up the loads.

'Over the second river by a suspension bridge, and then a whole day going up hill, very hot and steep, the hard trod clay very slippery. Higher up lots of water flowing everywhere, irrigating the brilliant emerald-green paddy fields and rushing down the paths. I bartered a piece of bread for a small lemon with a little boy. He was delighted, so was I. Wet my towel and hung it over my head, the ends tucked into my shirt to drip down inside on the principle of a milk bottle cooler – whenever it dried on top I just put my head under a water spout. It was delicious!

'We camped on top of the hills, rather like the South Downs but much, much higher with immense views in all directions over a tangle of hills wooded to the top, range on range, fold on fold, with deep valleys and all the lower parts of the hills terraced for little paddy fields. The scale of everything is huge.

'That night the Sherpas did a dance for us by the light of the camp fire, arms linked, a sort of shuffling back and a monotonous song – they are just like a lot of schoolboys, always cheerful and ready to joke, shouts of laughter when anybody slips on the wet clay. But their devotion and care is touching.

'My chap, Darwa Norbu, a veteran of many expeditions, is expert at bagging the first tent that goes up. He has my bed out at once from heaven knows where, slaps it in the tent, blows up my air mattress, lays out my sleeping bag, produces my kitbag and has everything fixed before anyone has a look-in, and woe betide us if we try to change tents. I have done my best not to have a camp bed as I prefer the ground, but Darwa is adamant, his Memsahib is going to sleep on a bed, and that's that. If I get rid of it another one is immediately pinched off someone else and appears firmly in my tent; evidently it's a matter of prestige so I've given up and sleep meekly on a camp bed.

'On Monday came to a nice clean river and had lunch where it swept round a bend. The fun was to hurl oneself into the water just where it swept through two rocks and down into an under pool, but one had to work hard for the shore to avoid being swished away altogether. Some locals, working in a rice field opposite, sat in an astonished row for over an hour. It must have given them something to talk about for a year. We paused at the top of a ridge after climbing a steep path, and saw against a deep blue sky a whole range of snowy peaks towering above the ranges of wooded foothills, the most lovely and thrilling sight.

'And greatest thrill of all came with the sight of two distinct snowy cones in the far distance, each with a plume of snow blowing off the top, Everest and Cho Oyu — I shall never forget that moment. After all one has read and heard about them, to actually see them and know they really exist![2]

'Our track lay along ridges with steep drops to rivers far below, then down through pine woods to the first real suspension bridge, two chains high over a rushing river and narrow planks suspended on wires with occasional gaps, the whole contraption wobbling in all directions. It was quite a sight to see the laden porters going across. We had lunch by the river and lay in the shallows like water buffaloes under our umbrellas. It was also washing day, most of us and the Sherpas too, scrubbing away at shirts and pants and socks, laying them out on scorching hot rocks to dry. The Tibetan Sherpas, who wear their hair long in plaits around their heads, washed their hair too! Pem-Pem has a terrific length of hair, right down to her knees. It's quite an affair having a river hair wash.

'We are shaking down very well, no crashing rows, we are all getting along very nicely. The Sherpas are much amused by the floods of French which reverberate around us at full pitch. One hears them imitating it exactly on the march, followed by roars of laughter.'

A note from Eileen Healey said she was suffering from blisters

---

[2] The Countess was misinformed. When I reached this same area on a clear day a month later I noted a wonderful view of ice-capped Gaurishankar (23,440 feet) dominating the sky-line as I trekked down to the river. Everest and Cho Oyu were still far away towards the east, and only visible to me on the ninth day of my trek. In his book *Camp Six* Frank Smythe referred to Gaurishankar as 'so often mistaken for Everest in the past'.

and admitting 'I underestimated this march'. She mentioned that everybody was writing letters because Claude said they had eaten two loads and those two porters could carry messages back to Katmandu. She recorded that Pem-Pem had said that *chang* (the local brew) sold by an old village woman was no good, but the *chang* in Namche was like champagne, and noted that Dawa Norbu had carried her pick-a-back over a river to save her taking off her boots and socks, but left her to wade the next one they came to. She also told of being soaked by monsoon downpours that threatened to carry away their overnight baggage dumps, grilled by scorching sun as they toiled up rock slopes, making nerve-chilling crossing of chain bridges over fast-flowing rivers, being plagued by leeches and being kept awake at night by crashing temple bells.

In her note Margaret Darvall described a moment of ecstasy, meeting a melon seller at the top of a long uphill climb after their second night camp at Dolalghat at the confluence of the rivers Indrawati and Sun Kosi. Afterwards, she wrote, they used the melon skins to wash their faces. A typical dinner menu was roasted corn, mushroom soup, chicken curry and potatoes, stewed marrow, stewed pears. Some nights around the blazing camp fires five Sherpas produced an extraordinary collection of string instruments to make rhythm while they sang of Tenzing and Everest and other great deeds of Sherpas. The women porters, generally as tough as their menfolk and carrying loads just as heavy, paused giggling at swaying bridges over mountain torrents until male porters took their loads across before returning to help the women cross.

These pleasant notes from the women were not newsworthy, confirming my refusal to sit in Kathmandu trying to report the expedition.

At this stage war threatened further along the Himalayan mountain range where the small state of Sikkim bordered Tibet, and I had to drop the women's expedition. An urgent cable from London told me to rush to Sikkim to cover the threat of Chinese invasion over the Natu La Pass and down into India. I flew via Calcutta to Bagdogra, an airfield on the edge of the Indian plains, and took a taxi to the Indian hill town of Kalimpong, where I intercepted Mr Uppasheb Pant, the Indian political agent in Sikkim, en route for crisis talks in New Delhi. He refused me a permit to cross the frontier.

Next morning I talked with a member of a Tibetan refugee committee who was married to the daughter of the Maharajah, Kumari Phunkang Shey, also known as Princess Coo-coo-la, and he telephoned his wife about my wish to enter Sikkim. That evening Mr Pant's deputy telephoned me from Gangtok to say that a permit would be waiting at the border post at Rungpo next morning.

My taxi followed the route taken by pre-war Everest expeditions on a road built by Indian army engineers, climbing through paddy fields and jungle ridges, bordered by thickets alive with rhododendron and gorgeous orchids where giant butterflies of rare beauty fluttered. At the end of the road was the Natu La Pass (14,390 feet), also known as Jelep La Pass. There I saw soldiers of the Chinese People's Army poised on ridges around the border, making no effort to conceal themselves. However, after a few days of tension the Chinese pulled back and the crisis was over.

On my way back to Nepal, anxious about lost time, I was delayed for a frustrating week in Calcutta before two crates of gear and food for my own expedition, despatched to Calcutta by sea weeks before and due to be delivered to me at the Royal Hotel, were finally released by Indian customs.

First the shipping agents swore my crates were not in the ship at all, but when they searched again they found them stacked on the dockside. Then it took six more days of chivvying to beat the bureaucracy. At the same time I collected the Union Jack sent by air weeks before. Despite all of it having been consigned to me in the independent kingdom of Nepal I had to pay 90 per cent duty to India.

Then I took all of it with me on the next plane to Kathmandu, paying for 370 pounds of excess baggage. At Kathmandu customs there was no problem. They told me, 'We do not charge for expedition baggage.'

Several packages of messages brought by runners from the expedition were awaiting my collection from the British Embassy.

Countess Gravina wrote from their tenth night camp beside a jungle hillside monastery at Setha, 'We all went off to bed, some to sleep in the monastery, some in tents. In the former one faces fleas, in the latter leeches. I chose leeches and we had a gay night.

'In the middle of the night there was hubbub in the tent next door, indignant squawks from Loulou Boulaz who had found two leeches inflated like balloons inside her pyjamas. There came floods of French execration. I shone a torch around my tent. A regular parade was moving in on me, some crawling up the tent pole to drop on my unsuspecting head.

'Then there were screams from Tenzing's girls, and so it went on all night. Margaret Darvall took the prize as usual. A leech attached itself to the end of her nose while she slept. That was a great success with the Sherpas. They couldn't stop laughing, although they had a dreadful night themselves.'

The sleepy-eyed women climbed next morning above the tree-line, and in the middle of desolate moorland met three Tibetan Lamas, who fled at the sight of ladies with Leicas. Only when the cameras were put away did they return and give their strange visitors a recital on weird string instruments.

Other comments from Countess Gravina included mention of 'the English ladies, unruffled and methodical, keep a well-mannered distance which doesn't go down well with the egalitarian temperament of Loulou Boulaz, who grumbles that the Ladies Alpine Club is always up at 5 a.m.' Loulou also complained that Claudine didn't help with the cooking because she could only manage scrambled eggs, adding, 'But Claudine is very attentive towards the female coolies, who carry their load of 30 kilos like everyone else and sometimes a newborn baby on top of that.'

Reaching the uplands brought the women to the edge of the land of the Sherpas, and they began sampling the local alcohols, *raksi* and *chang*. It seems they enjoyed these and Tensing's girls were promising that the Sherpa cellars would improve all the way along the remaining way to Namche Bazar.

Some were facing up to the hard march less well than others. Once, Margaret Darvall failed to turn up at the camping place hours after the others were all there, and her two British companions went back along the track to find her and escort her in. She told them she was in no hurry as she disliked their staple diet of hard-boiled eggs, cheese, onions and rice, and wouldn't mind missing supper.

Eileen Healey made most of one day's march in what she called her 'creation Claude Kogan', a swimsuit from the Nice salon of the leader. This was because she had failed to get her laundry dry after an impromptu washing session in a river along the route.

By this time the three English women were dodging Jeanne

Franco's company. Till then she had spent most of the march walking with one or other of them, picking up the English language insatiably and untiringly.

Another despatch, a brief one-pager from Countess Gravina, was dated Jumbesi, August 31st. She began, 'I seem to have mislaid some interesting bits about Swiss cheese-making on our visit to a monastery, but you haven't missed much. The party is in fine form. We're really getting fit now and taking the 16 days' march in our stride. If ever you have a chance you should make this journey sometime, it is really magnificent country.

'Each day is the same in a way but the country keeps changing and our camp sites have very individual flavours. The people are delightful, very friendly and cheerful. These expeditions must have brightened their lives considerably along this route.

'No more now, it is 2 a.m. and I'm writing this by the light of the proverbial guttering candle, sitting in my sleeping bag as it is chilly here for the first time. The sounds are more Alpine, the rustle of water in the river, no more cicadas and thank heavens only one leech so far. A horrified Sherpa has just put his head in to see if I am at death's door with my light on so late – they are touching in their care and devotion.'

The next despatches sent when the women were two days short of Namche Bazar told of the worst ordeal of all the rigours of jungle and mountain travel. Above the Dudh Kosi, the Milk River, which flows from the slopes of Everest, they were attacked by a cloud of hornets. Countess Gravina wrote, 'We were all covered and swollen with burning bites from the enormous brutes. The stings even penetrated our trousers.'

Eileen Healey noted that they had camped at Changma where Wangdi was born, and where he saw his mother who presented the village with a sheep and *raksi* to celebrate her son's first visit in six years. On September 3rd she noted, 'A very unhappy day – attacked by hornets. Colette in great agony. Claude was the only one to escape. The bites leave a queer headache feeling and pain like hot needles. Porters suffered terribly.'

On September 5th, the 15th day of their trek, Eileen Healey noted, 'From the Dudh Cosi river valley the track rose steeply. Margaret overtook me riding a pony which she said Gyalzen had insisted she ride. Then the path turned a corner and there was Namche not far away.'

Next day she noted, 'Nepalese porters paid off, and loads sorted. Claude horrified that we've eaten 1,000 kilos of rice, 24 eating it three times a day, but more obtainable here. I think the French had no intention of accepting an invitation from two French students[3] to tea, but the three English went and had really delightful English 5 o'clock tea with chocolate cake and not a word of French spoken.'

Claudine van der Stratten wrote to her mother next day, saying, 'We were invited to the home of Sherpa Gyalsen ... there was a Tibetan meal with *chang* (alcohol from corn), then dances and songs with the Sherpas. Namche Bazar (3,400 metres, 80 houses on the mountainside, no radio, no telephone) is on the edge of the inhabited world.'

They decided to wait in Namche Bazar for better weather before leaving for their five-day trek to the foot of Cho Oyu. During this break they took the opportunity to walk to Thyangboche monastery, a half-day's march further up the Sun Khosi river, not far below the Everest Base Camp. Close around were the snowy peaks of Everest, Ama Dablam and Lhotse to the west and Kantega beyond the river.

Claude Kogan sent an expedition postcard to two friends in the Nice mountain rescue service, Angelie and Vincent Tesseire, saying, 'From Namche Bazar, four days from the Base Camp, the expedition sends you greetings. After 16 days' walk we are still all in one piece. The monsoon hasn't finished and we are staying here for two days before we carry on.' (The expedition postcard, printed in Nice, carried a colour picture with the caption 'Women's Expedition to Nepal. Cho Oyu 8,180 metres'.)

They left Namche Bazar in good weather on September 10th on what Eileen Healey descibed as 'The most beautiful walk I've ever seen, flowers, scattered trees, an easy path with snow peaks above. Wangdi says we need four more porters to carry wood, and we have 172 already. Rain again at 3 p.m. and Claude warned that the monsoon was by no means over.'

On September 14th they reached the Tibetan frontier, marked by a tree branch festooned with flapping prayer flags, at the summit of the 19,050-foot Nangpa La Pass. Eileen Healey noted in her diary,

---

[3] Students of anthropology returning from Namche Bazar.

'One of the most exhilarating days. After climbing steadily for four days from Namche Bazar and camping last night on the moraine by the glacier we wended our way between *seracs* (pillar-like masses of broken glacier), and eventually climbing steeply up smooth crisp snow that gradually levelled out and slowly the long-awaited purple plains of Tibet came into view. Nothing marked the frontier but a branch stuck into the snow with prayer flags. Neither habitations nor Chinese soldiers were in sight on the other side. Cho Oyu came into view soon after we left the top of the pass.'[4]

Soon after descending into Tibetan territory they left the route regularly followed by porters carrying cross-frontier trade, to turn eastwards towards two peaks, one inside Tibet, the other, Cho Oyu, just inside Nepal.

They travelled for close on two hours across Tibetan territory before climbing back to the mountain threshold that marks the frontier, and dropping down several hundred feet to where Sherpas were already setting up their tents on level scree for their Base Camp at 19,000 feet.

A yak, laden with additional stores, accompanied the lead porters from Namche to the Base Camp, and when the women arrived they found the yak had been slaughtered and joints of fresh meat were ready for their first Base Camp supper.

The non-Sherpa porters were paid off, starting back without delay for the milder climate of their valleys. While the Sherpas spent the next two days gathering rocks and building drystone walls around the kitchen and the mess tent, some of the women sorted out food and equipment ready to be carried up to the first camp. Others stayed in bed suffering altitude sickness.

Countess Gravina wrote me a brief note dated Base Camp, September 18th, saying how difficult it was to write with cold hands and by candlelight. 'Am writing this looking out of my tent door on a real Christmas scene, all the tents covered in snow and a wisp of smoke curling up against a big ice cliff, the big peaks around covered in new snow and gentle but persistent snow falling.'

Thus well advised of discomforts ahead I went to see the Foreign

---

[4] Chinese security has since moved close to the pass where the women climbers crossed into Tibet to get around an ice fall that blocked their base camp from access directly from Nepal. In October, 2006 The Times reported that Chinese frontier guards had fired on a refugee party shooting dead two Tibetan nuns crossing the pass.

Secretary, Nar Pratap Thapa, to collect the promised permit to visit the Namche Bazar area. He temporised, and asked me to call back at 3.30 p.m. the next day. Next day I found the whole warren of the government secretariat deserted. Nepal's most distinguished poet had died and government stopped as a mark of respect. Next day was one of the numerous religious holidays when government and commercial life halts, so I had to mark time further.

When I finally met the Foreign Secretary we talked about various world questions before he told me my permit was ready. It was a relief to pocket a piece of paper I could not read containing the official seal of the Nepal Foreign Office.

My first need was to employ a government liaison officer just as proper expeditions had to do. I took on 24-year-old Ratna Kazi whose normal occupation was teaching arithmetic, and soon discovered his English was subject to frequent misunderstandings. Then I went to a one-room office under a board carrying the painted legend 'The Himalayan Society', local rivals to Tenzing's organisation, which shared premises with the Nepal–Russi Friendship Society. Sherpas and porters looking for work crowded the building and overflowed among the chickens in the street outside. I told the secretary, a young man speaking good English, of my needs.

Next morning, well over an hour after the expected time, Sherpa Chowang Rinzi came into my service. Besides being a veteran of the 1953 Everest expedition he knew Cho Oyu, having climbed there with a Swiss expedition. He was to prove a stalwart, but on first sight I was disappointed. He was dirty and quite unprepossessing. I gave him 200 rupees to shop in the bazaar for kitchen equipment and stores.

At the Nepal Bank I waited patiently while they counted out £100-worth of Nepal currency into a stack of 1-rupee notes almost 2 feet high. Higher-value notes would have been hard to change in the countryside where only the lowest value coins were in use.

It was a busy last day before my little expedition set out. I had to buy extra food and beg and borrow extra camping gear. The liaison officer, whom I had to pay his normal 200 rupees monthly salary, feed, shelter and kit out, had not figured in my planning.

So I was late for the farewell party hotelier Boris of the Royal Hotel threw for me in his elegant flat. We had a boisterous evening, ending up at the home of the King's youngest brother, known as the Third Prince, to hear his latest records from Hong Kong. His house was a fine new Western-style building with sentries and an old cannon at the gate.

At 6 a.m., just three hours after my farewell party broke up, Sherpa Chowang woke me up to show off his new kitchen gear, and by 8.30 he and eight porters were on their way. I wrote a story to cable after breakfast and had lunch with Colonel Jimmy Roberts, also hung over, for last discussions on handling the runners who would be bringing my stories to him, for passing on to the telegraph office across the road from the Embassy.

Then, with my liaison officer, I began my trek to Cho Oyu, almost a month after the departure of the all-women expedition.

Chapter Four

My Trek to Namche Bazar

It began to rain as liaison officer Ratna and I left Kathmandu on Saturday, September 19th, three weeks and two days after the women's departure, travelling the first stage in a Landrover in driving rain. I recalled that Madame Kogan had said it was lucky to set out during rain, and felt huge relief at leaving behind my world of cables, telephones, hotels and taxis, the world of Cold War and moon rockets where a British general election was just beginning, happy to enter a land of hand-threshing, temples and superstition, still in an age before the wheel.

Soon after passing our caravan of porters who had set out hours earlier led by Chowang and kitchen porter Sona, the Landrover sank into deep ruts at the bottom of Chowki Pass. The driver told us we would have to walk up the twisting track ahead. I shouldered my rucksack, heavy with typewriter, two cameras, binoculars, toilet bag, towel and bankroll, and began the long walk holding an umbrella. Stormclouds blotted out the low paddy-terraced hills, and soon the rain turned the track into a deep orange-coloured torrent. In the main street of Banepa, after more than five drenched miles, we splashed through water over a foot deep.

In a hurry to shed my heavy rucksack I reached the hilltop campsite half a mile beyond Banepa well ahead of Ratna, and took shelter from driving rain in the lee of a tiny Buddhist monastery. When Ratna arrived he spoke with the saffron-robed monk who lived there and we were invited to shelter under the gaze of a giant porcelain figure of Buddha. In this oasis of dryness, we shed our wettest clothes and sat by the door waiting for the porters with tents and food to catch up. Darkness came with still no sign of them.

A boy of about nine brought the monk a glass of tea, and afterwards joined the monk on his knees in front of the Buddha. Together they murmured prayers. Ratna, a Hindu, and Chowang had arrived before me and were moving around preparing food, but the monk and the boy seemed unaware as their chants continued. After prayers the boy, an orphan being looked after by the monk, was fascinated with my compass

Chowang and the kitchen Sherpa, a bright-eyed youngster called Sona, built a fire in a sheltered place nearby intended for the use of travellers, and soon had piping hot sweet tea and an omelette ready. This proved to be a daily make-camp snack to keep the Sahib happy while supper, the main meal of the day, was being prepared.

At last the porters arrived out of the darkness, dumped their loads in the monastery and returned back down the hill to spend the night in town. The monk had invited us to sleep in his tiny temple, and as the campsite was waterlogged I was happy to accept. Supper came with welcoming warmth, tinned steak and kidney with boiled rice and fried potatoes and a kettle of hot tea.

By 8 p.m. I settled down in my sleeping bag, splendidly comfortable on a soft Lilo airbed. Ratna lay in his sleeping bag on an airbed nearby, and the little boy unrolled blankets, turned to me and put his hands together in the Hindu sign of *Namaste* showing his gratitude for a bar of chocolate I had given him. He settled down to sleep under the Buddha. The monk had shut himself into an inner private room. Mosquitoes zoomed around and bit me many times as I lay sleeplessly gazing at the Buddha, glowing in the flickering yellow light of a butter lamp. The boy slept peacefully. Ratna talked loudly and incessantly in his sleep.

Day 2: Banepa to Dolalghat

Chowang brought me a mug of tea just before 5 a.m. on a grey, forbidding morning. We ate breakfast of porridge, fried eggs and tea by candlelight, and prepared for the first full day's march. My rucksack was clearly too heavy for me, so Chowang wrapped my precious typewriter in a fur skin and stowed it on top of his pack. I was astonished to see a Landrover appear from a compound nearby. It stopped by the temple and a tall young American introduced himself as Dr Sturgess. He told me he had just established a missionary hospital there and was off on a once-weekly visit to Kathmandu, confident of getting through on a route local drivers refused to attempt. We shook hands and he drove off. I returned to travel as man has from the dawn of time.

35

It was drizzling finely as we walked eastwards through misty cloud over two ridges, and down steep slippery red clay slopes to another valley. By nine o'clock the rain had stopped and it was so hot that I paused for a swim in a broad stream, hopping out rapidly when a snake slithered from rocks nearby. Instead I washed and cleaned my teeth in a shallow pool. Army soap from my first compo-pack, black and unattractive-looking, lathered splendidly.

The way led across a broad valley, vivid green with rolling paddy and wheat, across a broad, shallow river by stepping-stones and over treacherously slippy clay ridges. The sun was shining from a cloudless sky and beat back from the clay slopes with baking heat. I took frequent swigs from my water bottle, and bought a water melon from a village shop and split it with Ratna. I ate my half gluttonously and l washed my face and neck with the skin.

I had been striding along well for five hours, but then the climbs became harder and going down steeply to a river valley my muscles began to hurt. While resting by a rushing grey river I spotted something basking on a rock, and through binoculars saw it was a jackal. The trail went on, it seemed interminably, switchbacking over ridges cut by streams, and along ledges reduced to as little as 6 inches by landslides after the previous day's downpour. At 1 p.m. I stopped for a bath in the grey waters of the river, but had to stay in a shallow backwater as there was a strong current. Afterwards I sat on a bank putting plasters on my blistered feet, as barefoot porters carrying produce for the bazaar in Kathmandu stopped to rest and look curiously at me. Desperately thirsty as my water bottle was empty, I filled it from a side stream, then had to wait half an hour while Halazone tablets purified it. Ratna and I waited two hours for Chowang to catch up, and discovered he had already had his lunch break. I had little hunger and after a few biscuits we pushed on with sweat pouring off us.

Parts of the track had slid into the river, and we had to cross landslides in soft earth. The river and its narrow V-shaped valley joined a river called the Indrawati, which we crossed by a 100-yard-long iron and plank suspension bridge. Soon afterwards this broader river, in its turn, joined the rushing, even wider Sun Kosi, the River of Gold. We crossed that by a similar bridge to make our second night camp in the village of Dolalghat. I could have walked no further that day. The last few hundred yards of level going were almost too much for me. I had done the last 6 miles on will-power alone with muscles crying out in pain at every step, especially the downward ones. It was excruciating, leaving me with no feeling for the magnificent scenery of wooded hills and spectacular waterfalls.

While Chowang produced tea and an omelette snack, I sat on a grass bank eating bananas. Chowang brought along a cockerel with a string tied to one of its legs, saying 'Six rupees, good?' We bought it for 5 rupees, but as we still had half a tin of steak and kidney to use up the poor creature was reprieved for a further 24 hours. It made the next day's trek in Sona's kitchen basket among the pots and pans that were to cook it! As next day's march would take us into a bleaker terrain we also bought a supply of onions.

The porters arrived just before dark and the tent loaned me by Boris Lissanevitch was pitched a few yards from the river with my ridge tent for Ratna alongside it. I watched a dugout canoe float past in the swift current. When my first aid box arrived I changed the sticking plaster on my crushed and bruised feet, and later limped stiffly to the few huts nearby. In what passed for the village store, an open-fronted house, I bought two torch batteries from a smiling woman with two naked babies around her feet. Although still near Kathmandu the batteries cost the equivalent of 4 shillings, more than a porter earned for a day's trek carrying a heavy load. It was wonderful lying in my mosquito-proof tent, but as I struggled into my sleeping bag rain pounded the canvas.

Day 3: Dolalghat to Nigala

I slept well until Chowang zipped open the tent doors with a mug of tea at 5 a.m. The rain had stopped and after a few hundred yards of stiffness my muscles ceased to hurt. The climb up steep red clay and tumbled rocks rising some 3,000 feet directly above the river was a killer, and the porters had to rest every 50 feet or so. On the way Chowang bought a bowl of bitter curds, wonderfully cool and thin enough to drink. Higher up still he produced the first bowl of *chang*, but it was too thick with corn for me.

At the top a woman sold melons, bitter tasting but thirst quenching. Chowang and I were sitting gloating about how well we had made it when Ratna, dead beat and moving at a snail's pace, joined us. When he had rested and finished his share of the melon, we went on over grassy uplands, still rising steadily, but comparatively easy going. It felt good to rest for lunch of tea, *roti* (unleaved bread), fried potatoes and bananas by a stream where I could wash and clean my teeth.

Then up more steeply over craggy moors to the summit pass, decked with ragged prayer flags, and down gradually through seemingly endless rhododendron woods as rain came again, and slippery red clay slopes to the next river valley tried my muscles savagely for the last three lip-biting hours. As darkness came with torrents of rain, we reached some scattered houses and I decided to camp. I could go no further. I had planned to camp at a place called Chyambas, where the women had camped the night after they left Dolalghat, and was under the impression we were still 6 miles short of it. We were in a place called Nigala and there was a note of despair in my diary entry that night: 'Must try to catch up tomorrow.'

Next day that I discovered we had passed Chyambas. It was on the top of downs far behind us, but thanks to Ratna's poor grasp of English he had not properly translated my wishes to Chowang. Two men and a boy in a shop asked us to join them in a glass of tea. It was warm and good. Then I sat shivering for two hours with no sign of the porters on the track above. Occasionally a customer would come from nearby houses for cigarettes or grain or kerosene. The cockerel was killed, cooked and made a tough, tasteless supper. The boy, who had been making polite smiles for hours surprised me by saying in well-pronounced English 'What time is it?' He had been swotting from a Nepali–English phrase book and had finally plucked up courage to try it out.

Earlier that day I had seen four men struggling over the trail to Kathmandu carrying what appeared to be a body in a hammock strung along a larch pole, and we learned they were carrying the boy's mother to the new American hospital at Banepa. She had been in a coma for four days with enteric fever. I revised my plan to sleep in the shop and when the porters with my tent arrived at 9 p.m. I had it pitched on sodden ground by lamplight.

Day 4: Nigala to Chitra

I had to wake the porters myself, missing my wake-up cup of tea because Chowang overslept too. It was 6.30 a.m. before we got on

38

our way, having seen all the porters off. The trail went painfully down to a fast-flowing river, and I took off my boots and socks to ford it, affording great laughter for passing porters carrying chickens to market as I balanced to dry my feet and get my socks back on. That valley was swarming with leeches, and when I took my boots off later I found one had feasted well on me. Sticking plaster was the only thing that stopped the prolific bleeding when a leech was pulled off. I also put sticking plaster on a raw 5-inch sore in the small of my back where my rucksack had been rubbing.

By the time we had climbed over the next ridge to another river it was so hot that I stripped off to bathe in the icy water, my first bath in two days. That refreshed me to take the next ridge in my stride. At the top we came to a big monastery and lots of banners and flags on tall poles, and was cheered to find this was Lishengo or Risingo[1], and that I was within two hours of being a day's march ahead of the pace the women had set on their approach march. Because of confusion over names the day before we had covered almost two days' march in one go.

On another long descent to yet another gushing river crossed by rickety, swaying bridges, my legs nearly failed me. An Indian policeman passed by while I was resting. He was on his way to a remote radio station, and he offered to massage me with oil, something I had overlooked when I drew up my medical kit. The massage was excruciatingly painful, but it was a godsend. My Good Samaritan was travelling with his son, aged about ten, who shyly accepted a packet of Spangles, from a store of sweets I carried for just such an encounter.

On the trail again we came to a pleasant riverside village, Deorali, among orange and lemon groves, and then climbed out of the blistering sun into cloud. The trail led steeply along a narrow rock ledge in the mountainside above a drop of thousands of feet. As rain started to fall I stripped to the waist to take a refreshing shower, but it soon turned to hail. We sheltered under an overhanging rock as hailstones as big as small pebbles bounced around.

The track broadened into a rocky staircase through rhododendron forests as black clouds blotted out the light, and the earth

---

[1] Places often had two names or more.

seemed to shake with thunder as the heavens opened. The forbidding darkness was momentarily cut by huge forks of lightning stretching from horizon to horizon. The track became a raging torrent, in places almost knee-deep in water, and it was a hard struggle to prevent oneself being washed away and swept over the precipices below. The storm cleared as quickly as it had started, but we were soaked through and frozen when we reached the shelter of a little hut near the summit. Then came a short descent to a collection of huts called Chitra just before dark. I sat on the terrace of one of the houses while Chowang lit a fire in one corner and produced the usual welcome tea and omelette.

A girl of ten or so emerged from the smoke-filled darkness of the cottage, moving on her bottom propelled by arms and one leg, holding her other leg in the air. There was a dirty cut under the toes and the foot was horribly swollen. I had never seen anything so badly infected. A piece of string had been tied around the leg in a pathetic attempt at stopping the spread of the poison. I felt helpless, thinking that the girl would probably die without hospital treatment. As I was regarded as a Sahib I was expected to be able to do something. I could do little that night as the porter carrying my first aid box was later than ever, arriving just before 10 p.m. I had already got into my sleeping bag on the terrace for warmth until my tent was pitched on a patch of filthy ground opposite the house.

Day 5: Chitra to Kirantichap

After breakfast I ordered water to be boiled, sprinkled iodine drops into it, and told the little girl's mother to clean the wound. She tried to put aside the cotton wool I provided and clean the wound with a dirty feather, so I had to clean it myself. Then I put on an antiseptic bandage spread with penicillin ointment and bound it around the foot and lower leg. To complete the treatment I gave the poor girl, who had sobbed through the pain of washing, a bar of chocolate, and hoped the village would not blame me for her death when I passed on the return march.

Our start was delayed anyway because three porters had slept back along the trail, and one of them limped in with a swollen leg. An old injury had opened up and he should never have set out. I

40

sent him back to Kathmandu, and Chowang found a villager who was prepared to carry his load onward for a few days. Another porter wanted to return, but changed his mind when Chowang advised me to demand back 20 rupees advance on what he still had to earn.

After consultation with Ratna and Chowang I also announced that from now on porters who failed to reach the campsite by 6.30 p.m. would be fined 1 rupee. The trail wound steeply downhill to a distant river cutting the next valley in a sharp V-shape. When we reached it at last we crossed on a single plank with chain handgrips, swaying fearfully over a rushing grey cauldron of water. While we rested on the river bank Ratna picked *umbala*, small, bitter, green fruit the size of marbles with a large stone, which helped prevent thirst, and Sona gave my legs a massage before we tackled the gruelling climb ahead.

As we passed a narrow waterlogged lane between paddy fields I saw two bearded Europeans approaching, and guessing they were two French students the women had mentioned in notes to me in Kathmandu. I greeted them, 'Comment ca va?' They introduced themselves as Michel Peissel and Alan Thiollier, and said they were returning from the Namche area where they had studied anthropology. It was their 41st day since leaving Kathmandu. They told me that they had looked forward to meeting the women's expedition, but they had had a cool reception, especially from their compatriots. They had made a chocolate cake and invited the women to tea, and only the three British women turned up. They said they had the impression that the women resented European males as intruders in the area of their mountain, and reckoned I was in for a hard time. We chatted at the trail-side for half an hour. I told them that the Russians had sent a rocket to the moon, which they found hard to believe. As they were short of food I gave them a few tins to help them through the last few days of their trek.

I was deadbeat when I followed my caravan through paddy fields to a pleasant camp at Kirantichap, where our tents were already pitched on grass opposite a few cottage shops. I wrote a story and letters to send down to the Frenchmen's camp, with a request for the letters to be posted and the cables to be handed to Colonel Roberts at the British Embassy. It was hard going with the typewriter balanced on ration boxes while I sat on my bedroll with a hurricane lamp perched on another box. I sent a story about meeting with the Frenchmen and of the brush-off they had received from all but the English climbers, adding, 'The Frenchmen tell me there is no need to hurry. Bad weather in the shape of snow on the slopes of the mountain will keep the women hanging about for some time.' One of the porters volunteered to earn a bonus of 10 rupees to take my messages two hours back down the trail in darkness, and brought back a pleasant pencilled note.

In four days I had covered the ground it took the women five days to march. It had been agony all the way, and I resolved to cut my pace to the same march as the women over the next few days. That was, anyway, the same daily marches as male expeditions made, a stage pattern laid down by the need to provide shelter for porters. My aims were inverse to those of mountaineers. For me the steep climbs to the ridges between river valleys were a relief from going down.

Day 6: Kirantichap to Yaksa

After breakfast a village woman wanted medicine for a pain in the chest, and I had to stop her undoing her blouse by giving her four aspirins with instructions to take two before sleeping that night, and two the next night. I thought it could do little for TB, but might make her feel better. The trail led steeply down through pine forest to a river crossed by a very good suspension bridge labelled with the builder's name, John Henderson & Company of Aberdeen.

In a village on the climb beyond it Ratna spotted water melons growing and we persuaded the owner who was reluctant to part with them to sell one for half a rupee, double the price of the previous one we had bought two days back along the trail. My muscles were beginning to get attuned to the march, and I became more aware of other things than the teeth-clenching rigours of trekking. There were butterflies of all colours and varying sizes – one beauty as big as a sparrow – and myriads of dragonflies and many lizards. Once I came across a large monkey, face to face on a narrow track, before he scampered away. Another time a giant brown eagle soared majestically a few feet above me. I also caught my first glimpse of the grandeur of the Himalayas as they can only be seen from close by on the ground. Cloud lifted for a spell from

42

the giant face of ice-capped Gaurishankar, towering 23,440 feet above pine woods.

After the heat of marching up a river valley most of the day we climbed 600 feet to the village of Yaksa, and a campsite just beyond. I had developed pain in my right leg and hobbled the last stretch. The porters arrived just before 6.30 p.m. and my tent was pitched before dusk. Rain drummed on the canvas all night.

Day 7: Yaksa to Those

We climbed a steep ridge, descended to a river crossed by a swaying bridge, then steeply up through leech-infested jungle to a windy, cloud-wreathed ridge, where we met two *dak wallas*, mail runners from the women's expedition. At first they refused to hand over the package addressed to me which they were carrying to Colonel Roberts at the British Embassy, but eventually Ratna persuaded them to hand over the thick wad of notes written from the women's Base Camp. I sat on a rock to read the pencil scrawl on tissue-thin paper, and then rested my typewriter on a *chautari* wall (built for porters to rest their loads without taking them from the harness) to send back another story.

There was not a lot to write about. Altitude sickness had hit most of the women at Base Camp. Even the energetic Countess Gravina was doubting going high herself because she felt so rotten. I was cheered by her comment that Eileen Healey had been chosen as one of the three likeliest to 'go high', for she was the only one likely to give me full co-operation. Eileen Healey wrote, 'The biggest hazard of life in Base Camp is bed sores. Because of the intense cold we spend 12 hours of every 24 in sleeping bags.'

These notes from Base Camp contained another pointer to poor planning. After paying off porters at Base Camp the women had just 18 rupees (about 27 shillings) left, and had to borrow from well-off Sherpa families in Namche Bazar to do that. The runners carried an SOS for funds left in the bank at Kathmandu.[2] As the runners sped off towards Kathmandu with my cables and letters, we went down to another river, crossing it and recrossing it over

---

[2] This story about altitude and cash, dated Friday, September 25th, arrived in the *Express* office in Fleet Street on September 29th at the same time as an earlier story sent on September 23rd.

single tree-trunk bridges, and stumbling over hazardous diversions where landslides had carried away the track.

This was my worst day. My boots were full of blood from leeches, and my right leg folded under me and I nearly collapsed. I noted in my logbook, 'It's amazing what the mind can force the body to do!' Faced in the late afternoon with a steep climb rising almost sheer from the river, I rested while Sona massaged my leg for ten minutes. Then I took the climb at a fair pace, and made the long descent to the Jokalanga Kosi valley and to the town of Those, also called Meksin, the halfway point to Namche Bazar.

Tents were already pitched when I hobbled into camp at dusk, for once far behind the porters. I washed my feet and weary legs, ate my share of a chicken that cost only 2 rupees with baked beans and soup, then against the noise of temple bells and gongs I read John Masters *Far from the Mountain Peak* until 9 p.m. I awoke at 1 a.m. to great crashes of thunder, battering rain and flashes of lighting that lit up the canvas. I heard people running nearby and shouting, frightened their precious few acres of paddy would be washed into the soil-devouring river. I spent the rest of the night dozing while trying to keep my sleeping bag above the torrent racing through one side of my tent.

Day 8: Those to Chyangma

Our march took us through the large village of Those, then came much hazardous fording of the fast-flowing swollen river and many side streams because tree-trunk bridges had been washed away; and scrambling over soft earth and tumbled rock where the riverside track had been carried away altogether. It was a relief to climb out of the baking river valley, steaming like a Turkish bath in the fierce sunshine that followed the terror of the night.

At a long lunch stop we dried out all our sodden clothing, the tents and other gear. I picked six leeches from my boots, and the greengage jam we ate with hard tack biscuits attracted a plague of wasps. Two hours after setting off again we were in thick swirling cloud. This made even more forbidding the religious tablets in the shape of elongated tombs placed at the summit of most major passes under a flutter of prayer flags. They all carried the engraved

44

mystical legend 'Om Mani Padme Hum' (Oh, the jewel of the lotus). Rain came again, turning the downward track into a turbulent stream as we came out of dark woods into a broad, grassy valley and to Chyangma, the first human habitation we had seen since early morning.

I was offered a straw mat in the outer room of a big house where a platform of board was raised above the mud floor, and slept there with Ratna and two household goats. Chowang and the porters slept in the other room with the family. The woman of the house was brewing *raksi*, the local liquor, and I drank some warm and found it not at all bad. There was a postcard-sized picture of the Queen – our Queen – on a shelf, and I was told it had been brought home by a family member who had served with Gurkhas of the British Army in Malaya. Plastered on an outside wall by the door was a petrol efficiency advertisement – a strange thing to find a week's march from the nearest internal combustion engine. Any scrap of paper had charm for simple people untouched by all the wonders of the modern world. I found them full of curiosity. They stared at me with frank interest and fired questions at Ratna and Chowang, inquiring every detail about me. Sometimes on a lonely track a grizzled, bent old man would straighten up and snap off a regular British Army salute as he muttered a greeting. They were retired Gurkha soldiers, whose combined pensions were Nepal's biggest item of foreign exchange. Since the third day on the long walk I had been puzzled by people asking whether we had come from Nepal. Ratna explained that outside Kathmandu valley the seat of government was known as Nepal.

Along the way I was getting used to being shown nauseating sores and rashes and horrible lumps bulging from places in the abdomen where no lumps should be. I could only offer aspirins, as being better than turning them away without the Sahib's medicine in which they had such pathetic faith. I like to think it did them some good psychologically, anyway.

It's a wonder I wasn't ill myself, for Chowang had no idea of hygiene. I could not get him to stop wiping my cutlery on his sweaty, greasy bush shirt as the last ritual before handing them to me, a sort of final polish. I partially solved the problem by giving him a clean bush shirt of mine. I also had difficulty in getting him to understand that canned rice pudding needed to be served on clean plates, not on plates I had just eaten meat from.

45

Day 9: Chyangma to Setha

The porter from the village where I had treated the little girl, since identified as her father, complained of knee pains and I paid him off his 20 rupees with a rupee bonus. Chowang replaced him with a man from Namche Bazar, only too pleased to earn 10 rupees a day and have company on his journey home. The other porters asked for an advance, and there was loud argument when I refused on the grounds that they had not yet earned their earlier advance. To set out from this comfortable lodging place I put on my expensive Italian climbing boots for the first time, for we were about to climb into the land of the Sherpas, the Sola-Khumba region of Nepal where the people were of Tibetan stock and followed primitive Tibetan customs.

We set off through the last tropical valley where the jungle was swarming with leeches. At another long lunch stop we finished drying our wet gear. I washed myself all over, washed my hair and put plaster on seven wounds inflicted by leeches. Scores of green and brown lizards popped out of nearby rocks to inspect us. Chowang and the other Sherpas were singing happily about the joy of returning to the high valleys where they were born, but the Kathmandu porters were glumly apprehensive and began putting on extra clothing they had carried bundled with their loads.

We climbed steeply for hours through a forest where the trees were stunted, looking like a petrified forest, gloomy and primeval enough for a pterodactyl to have caused us little surprise. But all I saw were giant kites soaring above and tawny birds like chaffinches with head feathers like a guardsman's busby.

High above the river, far short of the 12,000-foot summit of the ridge, we camped at the monastery at Setha, a large building, well built in stone with well-paved terraces. I decided to sleep under a roof again, and chose the balcony of a grain store. I did a bit of typing there before darkness came, and this fascinated the farming family whose guest I was. Below, a girl in Tibetan dress stopped flailing grain in the courtyard to give me a smile. An older woman, apparently her mother, was busy at a cooking fire in the smoky living room that led off one end of the balcony. The head man was staggering around drunk, and was embarrassingly friendly. Later Ratna told me in his quaint English that the hospitality available included the comfort of the women if I desired it. I told him to express my thanks but to pardon me on grounds of my extreme fatigue.

Day 10: Setha to Jumbesi

We were off before 6.30 a.m., climbing for several hours before the track levelled out through lichen-covered thickets covering a broad summit ridge. We were higher than all the ridges to the south and west, and back along the trail we could see fold after fold of the ridges we had crossed. The valleys were covered with cloud, but we enjoyed bright sunshine. The air was fresh and keen, and breathing became more laboured. The Sherpas whistled to offset, they believed, the effect of altitude. The summit of the ridge called Lanjura Bhantiyang Pass was dismal indeed, with stunted trees and ghostly shrouds of cloud. I was happy to find I made the steep descent beyond without much pain and at a good pace.

During our lunch stop I saw my first yaks, Tibetan cattle. A small herd passed single file along the trail, going the way we had come from. Our track led through fir and pine, where I saw several wild peacocks, to the grassy Jumbesi valley. We passed several neat timber farmsteads before reached a huddle of houses around a stupa (a memorial shrine) on the edge of the river. Here, just as rain began again, we found shelter in a two-storey house where the hostess, wearing Tibetan dress, hung grass to dry from a balcony and spread rugs for my comfort. For the first time I had strength to put my boots on again after resting, and explore the tiny town. There was a scruffy temple, the egg-shaped stupa, ragged prayer flags and white banners. The village was like a farmyard with cows and hens and goats browsing and pecking in refuse thrown from house windows.

Supper included a Sherpa dish of atta flour (like strips of spagetti) boiled with the green of spring onions. Afterwards I tried to type up some notes, but this brought the whole town crowding around me and the smell was simply too much! After consultation with Chowang using a few words of English, some of the Sherpa expressions I had picked up and some sign language, I decided that next day we would take a short-cut over a 17,000-foot pass (far higher than the summit of Mont Blanc, Europe's highest peak) to cut another day off the normal five-day trek from Jumbesi to Namche.

Day 11: Jumbesi to Phudawa

I took my usual daily pills (Paladrin against malaria, salt tablets and multi-vitamins) with breakfast porridge and omelette. Another porter was replaced by a local, the third change, but they were all away by 6 a.m., a record early start. We followed the stream high up the valley, instead of skirting the high ridge along the valley of another stream that joined the Jumbesi. High upstream we turned for a direct assault up the ridge.

There was no track, just a steep hillside covered with edelweiss, grass and bracken with clusters of firs – altogether prettily Alpine in the sunshine. Clouds rolled up as we climbed higher through dark woods of misshapen stunted trees, and on above the tree-line through sand and stone and rock rubble, broken by occasional soft carpets of edelweiss, blue anemones and even daffodils. We stopped for lunch among cold moss-covered firs in a sheltered fold. Then we climbed up and up and up to a wind-blown gravel ridge called the Doras Pass, above clouds that hid whatever was on either side. At an altitude higher than the Alps we followed the ridge for hours, with the sun sometimes breaking through the overcast to give glimpses of snow peaks close around, seeming almost close enough to reach out and touch.

At last we began the descent along boulder-strewn streams until we came into a broad valley a few hundred yards below the ice-fall of a peak that Chowang said was called Dudh Kanga, Milk Mountain. As we pitched camp beside the stream that began at the foot of the ice cliff, the sun broke through giving a wonderful view of the mountains hemming us in. I washed in icy cold stream water and felt life was good.

After dumping their loads the porters climbed to a cave, where they kept a cooking fire going all night to keep from freezing. Chowang told me the valley was called Phudawa, meaning the Valley of the Cave. Only then did I learn that porters had died from exposure here on an expedition some years before, and as a result expeditions since had all taken the lower trail where the pass was only 15,000 feet. I was the first white Sahib to travel that way since.

48

My camp in this wild valley was pleasant while the sun shone. I noted in my diary, 'Today's march about my limit again, my right leg giving odd painful warnings on the last stretch. It's been a tough one. I've just had a wash and cleaned my teeth in ice-cold stream. Surprised to find my beard is ginger.

'This is a lovely camp in absolute wilderness and the air is keen and for a change at this time, 4 p.m., the sun is shining from a blue sky. The fire is on for tea, but I wish my tent would arrive. A blanket of fog is already creeping down from the ice-fall at the end of a glacier.'

Later, I added, 'Tent pitched and rations sorted out just before dark as cloud like fog swirled around. Bitterly cold. I typed a little but hands were numb. After supper of steak and onions, boiled rice and tinned rice pudding all on one plate I turned in at 6.30 p.m. Read a few chapters and then soon asleep.

'Awoke shivering at 1.30 a.m. and slept fitfully.'[3]

Day 12: Phudawa to Chitre (Jungnasa)

My diary begins, 'Relief to get up shivering into my cavalry drill knickerbockers for the first time. Air keen and crisp. Numb with cold. Breakfasted crouching over cooking fire of bracken stubs; porridge, sausage and beans. Poor porters from Kathmandu, barefoot and in thin cottons, feeling cold terribly. Understand how one expedition lost two porters from exposure on this trail. Still in shadow of peaks though blue cloudless sky above.'

It was a delight to climb out of the shade into the sunlight, reaching a high ridge at 7 a.m. and shedding pullovers. The terrain of bare rock and blue ice pools, with the great snow peaks of the Chamsher Himal as a towering background, was exhilarating in its grandeur, and to the south ridge after ridge disappeared into cloud layers. A bird that looked like a peahen flew from under my feet as we descended a glacial valley to rejoin the expedition trail again.

We walked on through magnificent scenery of wooded ridges, followed a fault in the rock face of a precipice, and then on along a summit ridge that seemed to be on top of a world that stretched far

---

[3] It was lucky I found that my sleeping bag was inadequate for high altitudes in good time to hire heavy yak wool rugs at Namche Bazar before going even higher.

southwards to disappear in a blue haze. The scene changed rapidly as we plunged down through miles of dank, dreary rhododendron woods to Tanga, where three streams meet. I bathed in the icy water and had yak milk, tasting like curds, which Chowang had bought from a passing yak herdsman, with lunch. Then we climbed to a rocky ridge which the trail followed for several miles before dropping through more rhododendron woods into a fir forest on a steep hillside.

We descended to a place called Chitre, where there was a thatched-roof shelter provided for wayfarers. There was a constant roar from a river far below, and no level ground. My tent was pitched on a ledge too narrow for it, and part of it was left hanging. It was pitched just as rain came, and the hours till morning were a nightmare of rushing water. The whole hillside became a stream, gurgling through the tent and threatening to wash it away. Ratna slept well in his smaller tent, and Sona and the porters huddled together under the thatched roof with Chowang.

Day 13: Chitre to Juphede

It was cold again during the night, and I was glad to get up and dressed when 5 a.m. at last came. The rain had stopped, and we looked out on the forested ridge that looked so close, rising from the opposite bank of a river gurgling and roaring at the bottom of the narrow valley it had cut so deeply. The hour-long trail down was almost perpendicular, and so was the climb up the other side which Ratna dubbed 'our Everest'. The river bed was littered with huge boulders causing lots of foaming, white water. We crossed by a dicey tree-trunk bridge, and climbed the far bank by a tree trunk in which niches had been cut for travellers' feet.

The climb to the next pass took hours, and then began the descent into the valley of the Dudh Kosi, the Milk River, which flowed down from its source below Everest. Further down the trail the clouds broke, and I caught my first close-up view of the world's highest mountain, a thrill that made the trials of the long walk well worthwhile. Soon after that we came upon the first signs of human habitation we had seen in three days of travel, double-storey wooden houses, tiny fields and cattle. The cattle were, of course, that great shaggy creature, the yak.

Some miles further up the river we came to Juphede, a tiny collection of farms on a small plateau above the river, where I sheltered in a house between a cooking fire and a huge pile of stored potatoes until my tent arrived, for it had begun to rain again. Warmed by the host's home-brewed *raksi*, I began typing letters ready to send back with my next runners. The tent porter came in before dark, and my tent was pitched in a nearby field. Chowang and Ratna told me that according to village gossip three European women climbers had left the expedition's Base Camp because one of them was ill, and were lodged in Namche Bazar. My guess was that this had to be Margaret Darvall, who had been coughing when they left Kathmandu. In fact, only two were unable to take high altitude.

Day 14: Juphede to Namche Bazar

Rain was still falling from leaden skies as we set out on the last lap of the walk to Namche Bazar, and I wondered what problems this late monsoon weather was causing to the women on Cho Oyu where it would be blowing a blizzard. There was no pleasure in taking rest stops in the rain, and we passed the women's last overnight camp at Pem Garwa at 7.15 a.m. I pressed on as fast as I could across bouncy, unrailed bridges where the trail criss-crossed white water Dudh Kosi rapids as the terrain on one side or the other became easier, sometimes climbing high above the river to get around precipices falling straight into the torrent, then coming down to the banks again.

The scenery, later to be revealed to me as incomparably beautiful, was blotted out by rain. This was falling as raging blizzards around the snow peaks and was, I was to learn later, bringing tragedy to two women and two Sherpas on Cho Oyu. There was one last, long stiff climb up from the river before my goal, Namche Bazar, came into sight at 10 a.m. I had made it two days faster than the women. As I rounded the last bend the Sherpa capital appeared as an ugly collection of about 60 dwellings in a stark hollow, at 11,000 feet above sea level.

I was drenched and cold, but deliriously happy to have reached it.

Chapter Five

Women's White Lies

Dawn came clear and bright with the surrounding peaks a wonderful sight as my small expedition set out for Cho Oyu on Wednesday, October 7th. But mist came down as we reached the Bhote Kosi river after crossing a wide ridge from Namche Bazar. The trail along the river to its source near Cho Oyu was described by earlier European travellers as 'a dream of beauty', but it was hidden from us. We pressed on fast, reaching Thami, a pleasant little place on a rock ledge, in two hours although it was reckoned to be a day's march distance. Soon after crossing a col (a passage between areas of high ground) we came to a village called Changmuche, with lots of green camping places beside the river and many yaks still around.

At the top of chalk cliffs we came to a grassy plateau and a pretty, deserted village called Marlung, whose summer population had already taken their yak herds, goats and poultry to lower valleys for the winter. Chowang tried to get into one of the houses to do his cooking sheltered from a cutting breeze, but the roofs were weighed down with heavy boulders, the doors were padlocked, and the windows barricaded on the outside by piles of rock.

While waiting for the tent porters I wrote in my diary, 'Wonderful to be on the road again, to wash in fresh, clear, ice-cold streams and clean teeth properly. Cloud is just above our heads, but getting bursts of sunshine. Porters caught up at lunch, but when we reached the deserted village of Marlung at 2.15 p.m. they were far behind. Seems nothing for it but to camp here, though I would like to push on for two more hours of daylight. Since lunch the country has been very wild and stony, not even yaks about.'

The tents were pitched in a tiny walled field of grass beside a clear, icy brook, surrounded by rock faces with ice cliffs surmounting them and the peaks of the Rolwaling Himalaya. I put on gloves and stamped up and down to keep warm until piping hot tea and the usual omelette were ready. Darkness came early in the shadow of the peaks and for a change it was a cloudless night, a night of surpassing beauty under a crescent moon and stars that gave a tinselled effect to the gleaming high peaks all around. I sat by the cooking fire to eat supper, but by 7 p.m. it was so cold that I reluctantly forsook the beauty of the night for the warmth of my sleeping bag and the yak rugs I had hired in Namche. Life seemed grand.

Thursday, October 8th

Up at 5 a.m. to find frost on the tents, and we moved off over frozen turf at 6.30 a.m., feeling chilled at first in the mountain shadow. After two hours we climbed into sunshine and sweltering heat. By lunchtime the roaring river had slimmed down to a babbling brook, little more than ankle-deep in the middle of an alluvial cutting. I stripped in the warmth of the sun and splashed myself with freezing cold water. Wearing sun-goggles for the first time we left the friendly river, a last link with the warm lands below, and had to scramble over tumbled piles of rock and stone moraine left behind by glaciers. It was hard going with the sun glinting off the rocks, and I felt breathless, stumbling upwards rather than climbing. At noon we reached a sheltered defile, strewn with boulders as big as houses, at the foot of a granite precipice.

Beside a trickle of a stream we reached a camp site called Lunak with turf-roofed rock shelters built for travellers over the Nangpa La Pass to Tibet. As our porters were far behind, we left Ratna to make camp there.

Chowang and I reconnoitred the trail ahead – a lunar landscape of grey moraine, blue ice cliffs and a profusion of giant boulders – and saw that snow covered the trail ahead from far below the pass. The silence was broken frequently by explosive cracks among the rocks, and occasional roars like express trains as avalanches crashed down the peaks around, piling snow in great heaps along the edge of what seemed to be a lifeless valley. As we moved panting laboriously among the rocks, stones began to clatter around us, thrown by wild-looking men shouting and laughing. We sat on a rock regaining our breath as they climbed down to us, clearly thinking it all a great joke. They were on their way lower to

53

collect firewood for the Base Camp cooking fires, and said they had been told to keep any visitors away by throwing stones.

We returned to Lunak where my tent was already pitched and a merry fire was blazing. The sun was still shining at an angle just above the ridge of that narrow defile, but it was bitingly cold. Just before darkness the long-delayed runners arrived in camp, carrying as I knew the first news from the women addressed to me for more than two weeks. But the runners refused to hand the messages over as they said they had been told they had to be handed to the two Memsahibs lodging in Namche Bazar and to no one else. My Tibetan language chit of authority from Colonel Roberts was no avail, neither was the authority of Ratna as a government official. Argument, persuasion, bribery, threat of force, none prevailed. With so many of the expedition's wood Sherpas foraging near our camp, we were outnumbered. However, I had to admire the runners' devotion to duty, and hoped my runners would be just as unresponsive to attempts by the Byrne brothers to intercept them. These so-called Yeti hunters were in fact working for the *Daily Mail*, as I suspected.

Finally, I retired to my tent with Ratna to consider this new, critical situation. I felt very let down by the women, who had promised regular weekly reports with additional ones as events justified. Now they were trying to make their reports available only in Namche Bazar, as they had earlier tried to make them available only in Kathmandu. I decided to start out at first light and make Base Camp and return next day, but when Ratna heard from the Sherpas that there were no women at Base Camp as they had all gone to higher camps, I had to think again. This and the fine weather of the last 18 hours made it look as though the mountain might be climbed within the week, and that made the need to get a preliminary story back to London more urgent than ever.

There was nothing else for it. I would have to return to Namche Bazar to get the notes addressed to me from the runners, and despatch the news they contained to Kathmandu with my own runners by the next night. After supper I wrote a strong note to Countess Gravina threatening legal action for 'gross negligence in not fulfilling our contract'. I was having difficulty breathing, had a severe headache, and went to bed.

My log note written on Friday, October 9th, says: 'Hardly any sleep. Worry? Altitude? Probably both. Relief to get up at 4.40 a.m.

and be on the way in half-light by 5 a.m. Everything frozen hard. Bitterly cold. Narrowly missed coming a cropper on frozen stones across stream.'

I sent one of my runners to Base Camp with my note to Countess Gravina, and left Ratna, groaning with altitude sickness, in charge of the camp. Chowang carried my typewriter and sleeping bag and nothing else. We soon left the expedition runners behind, passing our Marlung campsite at 8.30 a.m. and an hour later the stream was a roaring river. In blazing sunshine it was a delight to see trees and other vegetation again.

Just above Thami we met two runners on their way to Base Camp, the same runners we had met six days out of Kathmandu, and they handed over messages and mail they carried for me, including cables sent by the office weeks before, one of them saying 'Max Aitken and Whitney Straight both asking how Claudine van der Stratten getting on. You might tell her they inquiring.'

A mile above Namche Bazar we met two runners of a succession Chowang had hired to join us, and they travelled back to Namche Bazar with us. The last mile was sheer agony, helped by fiery *raksi* from a water bottle carried by one of the runners, a smiling man named Palden who had a chit to say he was the Everest expedition's best runner. I made it painfully slowly down the steep ridge to Namche, and paused for tea in Palden's house, the first one we came to. There, sitting on a windowsill, I read the first news of the other world since leaving Kathmandu. While waiting for the expedition runners Margaret Darvall gave me some massage ointment, which I rubbed into my leg muscles.

The expedition runners came in five hours behind us, and at last I collected a bundle of notes addressed to me. They were useless, containing nothing after September 26th although the runners had left Base Camp on October 8th, some 36 hours before. I rushed back to the two women's lodgings to see if they had later news.

They told me there had been an accident and they would tell me all about it. Sherpa Chewang had been killed in an avalanche, but Sherpa Wangdi had escaped. They assured me that all the women were safe, and that Madame Kogan and Claudine had retired down the mountain from Camp Four and reached Base Camp safely between blizzards.

While I was typing this story we heard that the Sherpas were saying that two women were missing, which if true could only mean the two who had been at Camp Four, ready to assault the summit, when the blizzards began.

I went back to Miss Darvall and told her what the Sherpas were saying and she again assured me that all the women were safe. I had enough experience to know how wildly inaccurate Sherpa accounts could be, and I also felt that because of my special position with the expedition I had no alternative but to accept what the women told me.

Runner Palden and his son left at dawn with my story, and they made Kathmandu in a record five days,[1] winning themselves a large bonus. Such a pity they were not taking a proper account of the tragedy. After they left I went back to the voluminous diary notes from the women, written in ball-point on tissue-thin paper and impossible to read the previous evening by lantern-light. I typed out highlights from the diary of Countess Gravina, and from a long account in French by Madame Kogan. Then I went to say goodbye to the ladies before trekking back to my high camp.

As I was about to leave, Miss Darvall suddenly put her head in her hands, and said rather desperately that she was in an awkward position. Then it came out in a flood.

Madame Kogan and Claudine had been missing since October 2nd, and were almost certainly dead. The women had withheld this fact from me so that the next of kin could be told before it appeared on the news.

I noted the details and rushed with Chowang down the trail towards Kathmandu in an effort to catch our runners and complete my story with the dramatic news of the women's deaths. Far down the forested valley of the Milk River, breathless and bathed in sweat, we caught up with the expedition runners who had left an hour ahead of us.

They were resting at the women's Pem Garwa campsite while eating tiny wild peaches. They agreed to take my message and deliver it in Kathmandu inside six days for the bonus promised in my note sent with them to Colonel Williams. I sat on a river bank rock and typed a rapid story of the tragedy that I felt sure would make the front page splash when it reached London a week later. I wrapped it carefully in a polythene bag along with my rough notes

---

[1] This equalled Palden's fastest time when in 1953 he had carried James Morris's despatches to *The Times* with news of Hillary and Tenzing reaching the summit of Everest.

of the Gravina diary and several rolls of film for air-freighting from Kathmandu, and saw it stowed away in the runner's cummerbund before they headed westwards.[2]

Doubling back along the trail, I could now think of the loss of two women on a personal level, and was deeply sad to think that the trail I was now following for a second time had been a one-way journey for them. The exertion of catching the runners left us both weak, and climbing back to Namche was painful. We had only biscuits and chocolate to eat. As we paused to drink *chang*, sitting on a stone wall at a wayside farm surrounded by curious Sherpa children, a voice came in English, 'The *chang* here is good, isn't it?' A trader who had spent some years in Darjeeling introduced himself.

We reached Namche just before dark as yaks were being brought in for safety from prowling wild animals. While I was resting exhausted in my lodgings, a summons came to join the Lama for dinner, and I found I was not the only European guest in the little sanctum above a yak stall. Peter Byrne's brother, Brian, was already there trying to raise news on a radio he had brought. On it I heard that Harold MacMillan had become my MP.

The food, prepared by the Lama's womenfolk, was good though heavy, and more than I could manage even after the hectic exercise of the day. My plate was piled with what looked like dumplings but were minced yak meat inside atta flour pastry. With it came tasty hot soup. The Lama lifted a dumpling with his fingers, dipped it into the soup and then put it in his mouth. We did the same, and I found it most tasty. Over dinner Brian said his brother had left that morning for Nangpa La, intending to inquire into reports that the Abominable Snowman had been seen there. I asked him what newspaper they were reporting the women's expedition for, and he just laughed. My legs ached as I staggered back to my sleeping bag, but I made up my mind to get to Base Camp before Peter Byrne, even though he had had a day's start.

Sunday, October 11th: Namche to Tuksumba

In pre-dawn gloom I massaged my legs with ointment, put Elastoplast on a new blister on one of my feet, and rubbed in foot

---

[2] Unluckily for me, one of these runners developed leg trouble and they took nine days, a day over the normal time from Namche to Kathmandu.

ointment. Soon after dawn I was climbing above Namche with Chowang and two fine young Sherpas to augment my runner service. We passed Thami at 9.30 a.m. and passed Peter Byrne's caravan of 17 porters at 10.30 a.m. Just below Marlung I was hailed by Peter, who was sitting on a wall reading Alan Moorhead's *Gallipoli* while waiting for his porters to catch up. He walked with us, but was puffing and obviously finding it hard to keep up our pace. I was surprised that a man whom I presumed spent much time in the mountains was less fit than I. (I was thankful for a bad attack of asthma the previous winter which had prevented me smoking, and after which I never smoked again.) I had been hoping to make my high camp at Lunak to sleep even if it meant travelling in darkness, but Chowang shook his head at the prospect. As the sun sloped downwards over the peaks Chowang led us into a village called Tuksumba, hidden from the trail by a granite ridge, making it clear by signs that to go on would mean death from exposure.

We intended to break into one of the abandoned houses for the night, but by the time Peter's porters arrived it was so freezing cold I was glad to accept his offer to share his tent. He said he was paying off all except five of his porters and making that his base for the next two months while he searched for the Yeti. He denied working for any newspaper other than an American syndicate covering news of the Yeti. There was a long argument over the pay-off before his porters, including several women, accepted a compromise and went off happily to light a fire in a house where they spent the whole night singing.

Meanwhile Chowang and Peter's cook had a yak-dung fire going in a house near the tent and we enjoyed a feast of stew and canned pears to which our contribution was two small cans of baked beans and rice pudding. Peter and I also had rum and honey punch. This was a revelation of the difference a little more weight and several more porters can make to Himalayan travelling. We even sat in folding chairs, the first I had seen since Kathmandu!

Monday, October 12th: Tukzumba to Lunak

The sun glinted on snow peaks as we set out in the chilly shadow they cast, and saw the massive summit of Cho Oyu (the name

58

translates as Big Head) for the first time. We had just climbed into the welcome warmth of sunshine when we met the two runners I had sent up to Base Camp. They carried a letter written by Countess Gravina at Camp Two replying to my note of October 8th, and expressing concern at my feeling of being let down. With it came the latest news, already two days old, about the search for the missing women and Sherpas.

While my runners rested, I sat on a rock and wrote a detailed story of how blizzards struck as Claude and Claudine were at Camp Four ready to make a summit bid, and about the first efforts to find out their fate with the loss of a third Sherpa and the survival of Sirdar Wangdi. It was a first-class story, and I sent runners on their way with the promise of a big bonus if they delivered the messages to Colonel Roberts six days later. With their departure I had three separate runner two-somes on their way to Kathmandu.

When we reached Lunak, we found the rest seemed to have cured Ratna of altitude sickness, and the camp was in good order. I invited Peter to share my frugal supper, but he felt too unwell and had an especially early night in his sleeping bag.

Tuesday, October 13th: Lunak to Base Camp

It was a relief once again to get up and into action before daylight. After breakfast in the smoky shelter where the porters spent the night, I bid Peter farewell. When I looked inside his tent he was still unwell with altitude sickness and said, 'I shall just have to take it easy for a day or so.'

With relief, I followed Chowang up the defile of frozen turf and into the lunar landscape we had seen several days before. Soon after, the sun climbed over the peaks, Chowang indicated it was time to put on snow goggles and glacier cream. The effects of high altitude made following the track difficult, demanding the last reserves of dogged strength. Every movement took double the effort it required a few thousand feet below. Without the added handicap of suddenly being out of breath in the thin air, the sizzling glare of the sun and the terrain made it a test for the fittest and strongest man. No wonder the women had made the journey from Lunak to Base Camp in two short stages.

Our way twisted up, down and around great piles of rocks and boulders, ice cliffs, and blue ice pools, the surface of a sheet glacier older than history. My rucksack, stripped down to only cameras, notebook and spare pullover, got heavier and heavier.

Just before the snow-line we caught up with a huddle of porters on their way to trade in Tibetan villages across the pass. They had spent the night in a rock shelter just below the snow-line. One of them offered to add my rucksack to his load, and I thankfully took up the offer. I thought the demands on my flagging strength were almost over as we went up the broad saddle of the pass with my feet sinking only about 4 inches into the snow. But there was one new horizon after another, and it seemed to go on for hours. At last I saw the branch of a tree stuck in the snow to mark the 19,035-foot frontier. Prayer flags decking the branch were as stiff and lifeless as the land around. I floundered up to the branch and sat beside it. It was an exhilarating moment although I was numb with fatigue.

I spent a long time scanning the other side through binoculars. I made out two broken trails. One towards the women's Base Camp branched off to the right, and a wider track went directly north-wards to Kyetrack, reportedly the nearest Chinese check-post some 6 miles below. Rolling away in ridges of grey-brown moors lay the mystic land of Tibet, isolated in that wind-blown wilderness from the rest of mankind. This remoteness was its tragedy, for the world back along the long trail did not particularly care what I had learned in my travels, that the Tibet of prayer and contemplation was as lifeless under Chinese occupation as the frozen prayer flags on the branch brought up from the tree-line far below.

The snow-line ended only half a mile below on the sunnier Tibetan side of the pass, and the country beyond it looked far less harsh than the last 15 miles on the Nepal side. I saw no sign of a Chinese patrol, only the backs of the friendly porters plodding downwards. Rested and filled with the wonder of it all, I followed Chowang into Tibet. After half a mile on the main trail we turned off along a broken trail skirting the edge of a huge ice cliff and running parallel to the border. The going became killing as the sun had softened the snow and the effort was near heart-bursting as every step went deep into the snow. At last we reached a jumble of rocks at the edge of the snow-line. I was deeply conscious, despite the physical demands of movement, of the consequences of being caught half a mile on the wrong side of the watershed that marked the frontier.

We continued over tumbled rocks, ice and snow, crossing back over the watershed into Nepal, and Cho Oyu, the killer mountain, rose up massively ahead, glinting in the sunshine and casting a great shadow as the sun began to sink. There was no sign of a track or of a camp and we were becoming alarmed, until we were relieved to meet two expedition runners – old friends met with twice on the trail before – on their way back once more to Kathmandu with expedition mail. They directed us onwards. At last, close to exhaustion, I saw tents and human figures around them in a hollow below.

As I stumbled downwards over the rocks I made out the figure of Countess Gravina dashing around giving instructions to women and Sherpas. I wondered whether we might be met by a hail of stones, but we stumbled down over rocks and ice to the tents, to be met with warm greetings once the women recognised me under the growth of a ginger-tinged beard.

I pushed my goggles pushed back over my balaclava as I was ushered to a camp chair. Bowls of fruit juice and tea were pressed upon me as a burring cine camera recorded the occasion. Countess Gravina suggested I stay as their guest until I had all the information I wanted, a life-saver for me as it was already too late to return over the Nangpa La Pass that night. Cho Oyu was already casting a great shadow as the sun began to sink behind it.

The Sherpas pitched a tent they had brought down from Camp Two for me to sleep in, while Chowang bunked with his Sherpa chums. The women found me a spare duvet suit since they said the plunging sub-zero night temperature would be colder than my Alpine clothing was meant to withstand.

Sipping a mug of sweet tea, Countess Gravina, who had returned from closing down the lower camps only the previous day, told me of her frustration at the sad end of what, at her age, she considered her swansong among the high peaks, especially as she had far surpassed her own altitude expectations and felt she might have gone higher still, even perhaps to the summit.

She said, 'I wanted to try to keep on trying for the summit so that we might make it a crowning memorial for Claude and Claudine. But the others thought we should leave Claude with her altitude record. She won it five years ago on this mountain and this

61

is where she is buried. So we are going to pack up and go home. It's a shame as the weather now is just right for a go at the summit.' She sighed deeply, and added, 'If only they had not been in such a hurry.'

Jeanne Franco told me, 'Everybody says Cho Oyu was much too high for our expedition, but enough of us had the possibility of getting to the top to justify it. With two nights at Camp Four, Mam[3] and I could have had a good shot at it.'

Sherpa Gombu, Tenzing's nephew, shook his head in the affirmative manner of people from the Indian subcontinent. He said, 'They should have sat out the weather resting at Base Camp. I have never seen such avalanches as those on October 2nd. It was an error of judgement, a mistake in estimating the weather.' Looking around at the sharp, glistening whiteness of Cho Oyu rising majestically into the cloudless sky, he added, 'With the weather now they could have done it. Claude and Claudine would have got to the top; maybe two of the old muttons and the girls[4] as well.'

Years later, in his book *After Everest*, Tenzing made this comment on the expedition in which his daughters climbed so well: 'As the expedition turned and headed back to Kathmandu the mountain shone bright and clear in a blue sky. Had they started for the mountain a little later than they did they might have succeeded without trouble. But that is the luck of the weather in the Himalayas.'

After dark it was bitterly cold as I walked from my small tent to join eight rather wild-looking women in a cosy little rock-walled shelter, crowded around brightly coloured mess tables. All of us, including the Sherpas, were clad in sky-blue padded clothing, and the women wore red and navy blue jockey-style woollen hats. I wore a grey balaclava. To a light-weight traveller like me it all seemed luxurious. I was given a chair at the head of the table. It seemed like a banquet – mushroom soup, frankfurter sausages and fresh-tasting juicy steak from the camp's natural deep freeze, the campsite ice pool. The last of their six bottles of whisky, donated by the Ladies Alpine Club, was opened. The shots were giant-sized all round for it was bitingly cold. Nobody wanted water mixed with it. We raised mugs and bowls for a toast in silk-gloved or mittened hands.

---

[3] Her name for Countess Gravina.
[4] Tenzing's girls.

I was surprised to find them so cheerful. The shock of the tragedy was behind them, worn off in the grim days of waiting till the blizzards ended. Countess Gravina, almost apologetically, explained 'Life must go on.' Sherpa Wangdi, sitting with huge bandaged hands in his lap and being fed by a Sherpa colleague, was a constant reminder of the tragedy. But he was as cheerful as any of them despite the great pain he must have been in. After supper we adjourned to the cookhouse – another rock shelter covered with a canvas fly-sheet – to warm ourselves by the smoky cooking fire. The Sherpas frying chapatti bread were some of Tenzing's Sherpa elite and I was thrilled to be in their company.

Around 7.30 p.m. the women drifted away to the warmth of their sleeping bags in tents scattered among the rocks. Tired as I said I was, Dr le Bret advised me to take a couple of sleeping pills to make sure I slept. My diary note says, 'I took off only my climbing boots before slipping into my sleeping bag, suspended above sharp rocks on a Lilo airbed, I kept my balaclava on and buried my face in the down, and slept till the twilight of dawn. This was my normal time to get up and I struggled out of the warmth, reached for my boots and found them frozen solid. I should have put them in my sleeping bag with me. Stepping gingerly in stockinged feet over icy rocks I picked my way to the kitchen and thawed the boots out while sharing the Sherpas' dawn cuppa. It seemed I was abroad too early, the Memsahibs not being in the habit of appearing until around 8.30 a.m. when the sun's warmth reached the camp. Jeanne Franco was the first of the women to appear for pre-breakfast tea and a snack of fried yak steak. A bit later I made a hearty breakfast of another yak steak and fried eggs, still having none of the usual symptons of altitude sickness.'

Sherpa Gyalzen left to fetch porters from Namche Bazar to carry the expedition's goods back to Kathmandu, and over breakfast Countess Gravina and Eileen Healey offered to accompany me in climbing part of the way up the mountain across the watershed in Tibet, where I would have a grandstand view of the whole of Cho Oyu and be able to trace the climbing route and pinpoint where the high camps had been right up to Camp Four. As we climbed up from Base Camp the sun was shining and the snow and blue ice and the great peaks around were a picture of remote, cold beauty. We scrambled over ice-falls and tumbled rock, mostly free of snow as it faced the full force of the sun for most of the day.

After two hours we reached a vantage point from where the summit of Cho Oyu seemed much closer than it did from below. Far below, Base Camp appeared minute. The Nangpa La Pass was far beneath us, and my companions estimated the height at well over 21,000 feet. This I knew was the highest a reporter had been in pursuit of a story at that time.[5] Almost the whole of the climbing route from Base Camp to the smooth snow slopes where Camp Four had once stood was visible. The great rounded summit of the mountain looked much less formidable and awe-inspiring from that vantage position. Through binoculars, every ridge and rock and every avalanche breaching the climbing trail stood out clearly.

Countess Gravina pointed out the line of rocks stretching across the mountain not far below the summit. Camp Four, the tiny tent in which the two women climbers and their Sherpa had waited for the storm to blow itself out before attempting the summit, had been pitched just above them.

This was close to the position Claude Kogan had reached on her earlier attempt with Raymond Lambert, presumably chosen in order to reduce the length of the final assault. It was 400 metres above the Camp Four site chosen by Lambert which was on a snow ledge, 900 metres from the summit, in the shelter of the rocks in case avalanches swept the face of the mountain. Below the rocks was a wide hollow. Above, the great face of the mountain showed bare rock faces, in this spell of warm sunny weather clear of blizzard-driven snow. Masses of snow from it must have crashed down and buried the occupants of Camp Four deep in the hollow below. Countess Gravina pointed out where the climbing route crossed the main face of the mountain, and the spot just below the grim-looking ice cliffs where Sherpa Chewang had died.

As we started down Countess Gravina repeated, 'If only we had waited for this good weather. I'm sure in the past few days we could have been making the summit. This must surely spell the end of women's expeditions, and I suppose I have been as high as I shall ever go.'

Below, like tiny black ants, we saw a party of Sherpas sent out to

---

[5] My record lasted till 1989 when Rebecca Stephens climbed to 23,000 feet on Everest while covering an Anglo-American expedition for the *Financial Times*. She later became the first woman to reach the summit. See Appendix Two.

64

search for a sleeping bag blown down from Camp Two as it was being abandoned. Both women expressed relief when they saw they had all moved clear of the lower edge of a great pile of avalanched snow in the shadow of the mountain.

I had enjoyed the climb in the keen air and sunshine, and was so ravenously hungry that I did justice to huge yak steaks for lunch. My climbing companions commented on my good wind during the climb and clearly envied my being able to eat so heartily. Jeanne Franco said, 'You were made to be a mountaineer.' I was most happy at that comment from the wife of a leading Alpinist.

After lunch I set my portable typewriter, my constant companion, on a table in the mess shelter and sat in a huddle with Countess Gravina and Jeanne Franco typing their accounts of the expedition's efforts and its tragic end. After typing details of the setting up of the high camps, the fatal blizzard, the rescue attempt that cost a fourth life and the retreat to Base Camp the women left me to talk with Wangdi, the Sirdar of the Sherpas.

He held a cigarette between his thumb and a huge bandage around his frost-bitten fingers, eyes dull with pain, but teeth flashing the good humour with which Sherpas seem always to regard the hardships of life in their harsh altitudes. He spoke in halting English, helped out occasionally by Sherpa Gombu, who was years later to be the only man to climb the summit of Everest twice.

This was his story. 'The Burra Memsahib (Countess Gravina) could not order me to go but I knew she wanted me to bring down the two Memsahibs from Camp Four. She said it was not safe, but I told her it was my duty although I thought the weather was too bad and it was likely to be several days before it improved. I decided to take Chewang with me and to go up without loads, intending only to bring the other Burra-Memsahib (Madame Kogan) and Claudine down. The snow was much deep and it was still snowing. It was hot with the sun glowing like a red ball through the snow clouds.

'We found Depot Three, then we came to the site of Camp Three where a sleeping bag was the only thing we could find. We rested there. I had led the way that far, and it was hard work breaking trail in deep snow. When we pushed on Chewang took the lead to give me a break. We were roped together, of course. By ten o'clock we were above the ice cliffs. Suddenly I felt a slight movement under my feet, and shouted a warning to Chewang. He laughed and said there were no avalanches.

'Almost at once I fell down and my ski sticks disappeared in the snow. I shouted to Chewang "Avalanche – stick your ice axe in." He shouted back "We are safe enough here." There was no noise except our shouts but the snow seemed to be moving beneath us. Next moment I saw Chewang rolling over and over in a river of snow rushing down the slope. I was pulled after him and remembered to cover my face with my hands.

'I don't know how long it was before I stopped moving, buried in the snow. My breathing melted a place in front of my face, and after a while I pushed my hands out and found they went clear of the snow. But I couldn't move my body. I shouted and cried and felt I was going to die. I could only move my hands. The rest of my body was firmly held. I remembered I had a knife in the breast pocket of my windproof, and eventually managed to reach it. Little by little I cut away the snow but I could not cut through the straps of my rucksack. Slowly I made more room, and struggled free to the rope around my waist. But I had lost my cap and my right-hand glove and my hand got frozen and I could no longer hold the knife.

'Finally I struggled free, and tried to take in the rope to find Chewang. He was buried too deep. I untied the rope and threw away my rucksack. I realised I would never make Camp Four even if it still existed: I had to go down for help to dig out Chewang. I took a flagstick route marker to use as an ice axe. I don't remember much else, only that I wanted to get down and find somebody alive, and knowing I had to keep moving all the time.'

Sirdar Wangdi estimated that he was buried about two hours in the avalanche, and that it was about noon when he began his lone descent of some 5,000 feet across the lower slopes of a mountain torn by giant avalanches.

Countess Gravina was glowing in her praise of him. She said, 'That journey down the mountain was an epic of endurance. Wangi is one of the bravest men alive.' In her diary she had recorded, 'Now I curse myself for not staying at Camp Two myself with a Sherpa to act as link. But at the time there had been no avalanches, and the two parties left on the mountain seemed so strong. As it turned out I don't know whether that would have helped, except to bring Wangdi down. Your judgement is affected at high altitude, but at that time we had no thought of disaster.'

It was contrary to the lore of Himalayan expeditions to allow a Sherpa, even a Sirdar like Wangdi, to take over the responsibility for rescuing those higher up the mountain. Any such task, inherently more dangerous than normal climbing, was conventionally undertaken by the most senior, fittest and most capable members of the expedition. Sherpas would normally have played only their normal secondary role, if any, both for their high-altitude experience and for their generally greater load-carrying abilities.

Climbers from distant lands pay the expenses and accept the risks of death and injury to challenge the world's greatest peaks. Sherpas went up to these hazardous high places for money. They were paid employees. Their motive was to raise the living standards of their families above the subsistence level of the yak and small-holding economy.

This new twist in the earning power of the Sherpa villages came at the turn of the 1950s when the Chinese People's Republic occupied Tibet, closing the traditional route to Everest from India through Sikkim and across the Tibetan plateau.

Before what soon became an annual pilgrimage of wealthy strangers from a different world, the people in the Sherpa villages never trespassed far up the highest slopes of the mountains that overshadow them. Only a few ventured over the 19,000-foot Nangpa La Pass to trade with Tibet. The towering peaks were regarded as the abode of the Gods and the lair of the legendary Yeti, superstitions that early Sherpa porters showed great courage in overcoming for the small sums of money the early expeditions paid. Such superstitions linger deep within the psyches of 'Tiger Sherpas' like Tenzing and the Sherpas he hired for the All-Women Expedition, nurtured from childhood along with ambitions to earn wealth by going high.

Their yak-herding upbringing was overlaid for the luckier ones with a sophistication picked up at Tenzing's mountain training school at the Indian hill station of Darjeeling. Wangdi's task, as chief of the high-altitude porters, was to oversee expedition logistics, to organise the lifting of equipment and stores to high camps under the supervision of expedition members. Such men are normally worthier of much more than their hire, providing invaluable advice to employers who earn their liking and respect.

The fact that for reasons of transportation of equipment and stores the high-altitude Sherpas mark routes, build bridges over crevasses, and cut steps in ice pillars, is a welcome boon to expedition climbers. Over the years this produced an elite of 'Tiger Sherpas' like Tenzing and his men who virtually became accepted as expedition members themselves, although paid. Wangdi knew the risks in his attempt to rescue the two women climbers and his Sherpa friend and colleague. He faced them because as most senior man on the mountain he felt the responsibility fell on him, as he made clear in my interview with him.

After typing these notes there was still time to sit chatting around the blue ice pools, glittering with jewelled brilliance in the late afternoon sunshine, in a bewildering mixture of English, French and Sherpali. I announced I was leaving next day, planning to send stories from Lunak, and a full detailed story of expedition from lower still. I believed I would be able to think and write better than I could at these really high altitudes, where my fingers burned with cold on the typewriter keys. I thought this might also lessen the risk of my messages being intercepted by the brothers Byrne somewhere below the Nangpa La Pass.

Moments after the sun sank out of sight, the temperature dropped below zero, and the women scattered to their tents for thicker, padded clothing, while I put on a borrowed duvet jacket in place of my nylon fur-lined windproof. Dinner was rather special. Jeanne Franco had been busy in the kitchen for more than an hour over the smoky fire, and the exquisite sauté potatoes she produced were delicious, a welcome change from Sherpa cuisine. We sat up late over the kitchen fire, and when I got into a sleeping bag along with my climbing boots I slept badly.

My diary notes say, 'The night seemed an eternity although I had taken one of Dr le Bret's sleeping pills. A little white creature, a marmot, pottered up beside my sleeping bag, took a look at my nose and then ran out of the tent, Wonder how they live this high. I've also seen a few giant black birds called Choughs which probably fly to lower valleys at night. Up at 6.30 after restless though not particularly cold night, to sub-zero temperature. Thawed my boots out at kitchen fire, breakfasted on porridge and yak steak with the ladies. They had all been busy by torchlight the night before writing letters for me to take with me to Namche and then despatch them to Kathmandu with the runners who carried my cables.

'I was on the point of telling them they would in fact go with my second runners because I suspected leaks to the Kathmandu freelancers from messages sent to Boris at the Royal Hotel, but decided they would not understand. I shook hands all round and departed rather later than intended, anxious about the condition of the snow on the pass if the sun had been on it too long before we crossed. The women pressed biscuits, chocolate bars and hot drinks upon us from their great surplus of stores, and with cine cameras whirring again we climbed the scree, turned for a final wave and pressed on.

'The snow was reasonably firm and we travelled fast to the Nangpa La Pass. From the prayer flags marking the frontier – one of the loneliest places on earth – we saw two other travellers coming our way. It was Peter Byrne, pursuing his Yeti hunt in the direction of the women's camp, with his personal Sherpa. This confirmed his interest in the women for another newspaper, and after the briefest exchange in a snow shower that had just begun, we parted in our different directions.

'Chowang and I went down the snow slopes rapidly as snow began to fall, then spent heart-bursting hours toiling over loose scree, tumbled rock cliffs and ice to Katuntangma where Peter had left a camp. Paused for coffee there and pushed on below storm clouds. I was feeling awful, clearly having taxed my strength to the limit. At one point I suddenly realised that I had lost all sense of danger, hopping from boulder to boulder without a thought about the long drop below. I stumbled and staggered on in a daze for hour after hour through snow and a keen wind. All the time avalanches crashed with roars like express trains down the mountain walls that hemmed in the rock-piled glacier we crossed. The tumbling snow made great piles like white slag heaps a few hundred yards or so on either side of our way.

'Driving snow whipped my face, and through the goggles I began seeing double. Several times I had shaking tumbles and narrowly escaped falling long drops by misjudging distances between rocks. For six struggling hours Chowang set a pace like a man possessed in his determination not to be benighted in that grim hostile place. Our only food was a couple of bars of chocolate, and the thought of my tent in the narrow defile among the rocks at Lunak became a mirage of comfort, always around the next rock face or beyond the next steep moraine[6] slope.

'At last – and only just in time – it lay below us, and somehow I picked my way through the last rocks to collapse gratefully in the shelter of my tent at 2.30 p.m. Ratna had spotted us coming and Sona had a comforting kettle of tea, biscuits and jam ready. I attempted to write the stories I planned to send off by runner next morning, but after trying to concentrate for an hour I gave up and went to bed.'

Friday, October 16th: Lunak to Thami

My diary note begins, 'Slept wonderfully for nine hours. Still warm and comfortable when Sona brought me tea at 5.30 a.m. Breakfasted on porridge and canned bacon in bed. Got up to find six inches of snow outside. Spent two hours typing, got runners away to Kathmandu with cables and rolls of film, letters of instruction about air freighting and requests to Colonel Roberts on what might be due in payment for the runners.

'We were on the trail in the tracks of the runners at 9.30 a.m. The fresh snow made the tumbled rocks below Lunak difficult, but when we reached the stream that later grew into the Bhote Kosi river the snow was melting fast. Strong sunshine had broken through the overcast. After two hours fresh storm clouds shut out the sun and there was a cold wind and flurries of snow again, but the trail downwards was easy most of the way.

'At Tuksumba, the Yeti-hunters' depot, its solitary watchman invited us to have coffee, and I'm writing this sitting luxuriously in a folding aluminium camp chair. Good to see walled fields and cottages again even though they're deserted.'

As we descended into moorland terrain the snow turned to incessant drizzle and we were soon soaked through. The roar of the river grew louder as scores of side streams joined it. It was good to see people living in cottages we passed as we approached Thami. It was 3.30 p.m. and I decided to stop in time to do more typing before nightfall.

Later I noted, 'My tent was pitched in a field edged by pine-

---

[6] A ridge formed by rock and stone deposited by a glacier.

woods which I thought looked comforting as well as pretty. I washed my face and cleaned my teeth for the first time in six days, and was just getting down to typing when Brian Byrne poked his head through the flaps of the tent to invite me to join him for *chang* in the house where he lodged. I joined him there and he came to dinner in my tent. He told me that he and his brother had been sending messages by runner to a representative of the *Daily Mail* (my old chum Larry Atkinson, the *Daily Mail*'s New Delhi stringer) who was waiting at the railhead at Dharran Bazar, a British Army Gurkha recruiting station on the Indian frontier. He admitted trying to nobble several of my runners for information, but said they had been stalwartly loyal to me.

'It became clear during an evening's conversation that he had little idea how the tragedy really happened, but he said he had sent off a message to say there was a rumour that two women were missing, but this was apparently not until a couple of days after my stories had been despatched.

'As I believed [wrongly] that Dharran Bazar was about the same distance in day's marches as Kathmandu I was confident I had no need to worry over this typical *Daily Mail* spoiling operation.'

Saturday, October 17th: Thami to Namche Bazar

My diary note began, 'Slept fairly well despite this latest worry. Chowang and I were up and away before Brian Byrne was astir, leaving Ratna to get the porters on their way. The cloud lifted enough for me to see how fabulously beautiful Thami was, nestled in a scenic pine-edged hollow among almost vertical snow peaks. But there was no time to linger. Reached Namche Bazar by 8 a.m., had tea and rusks with Margaret and Loulou, called at the Indian check-post. Began typing at 9 a.m., and in nine hours at the typewriter knocked out two news stories, a three-piece series by Countess Gravina, and a piece by Sherpa Wangdi, and wrote several letters.

'The Nepalese Major came to dinner wasting precious soup and meat as he is Hindu and vegetarian, he must have a hard time in the land of yaks. Thought he would never go, stayed on so long talking of his days with the British Ghurkhas. After he left I went back to the typewriter. Very late in bed – 10 p.m.'

71

Sunday, October 18th

Namche Bazar: 'Up again at dawn to see two runners off carrying my stories and the women's mail, which I had purposely withheld from my first runners because I felt sure [correctly as I knew later] that Boris was leaking quotes from letters he received to the correspondents of Indian newspapers in Kathmandu in exchange for them mentioning the Royal Hotel.

'I went back to bed after the runners left, but the habit of early rising was with me and I was in the Indian check-post at 8 a.m. listening to the news in English on All India Radio. The radio announced the news of the tragedy to the expedition, the news I had despatched eight days before, and it was so like my wording that I felt sure it was based on my stories published in the *Daily Express*.

'It was strange to hear something I had written some eight days before as the first item on a news broadcast. I felt confident that the runners carrying my story had reached Kathmandu the previous Friday and that my story had appeared in the paper in London that morning, doubtless a front-page splash. Unless very unlucky I should have had a scoop.'

Chapter Six

Author's Side Trip to Everest

After despatching my runners with brief accounts of events described in the last two chapters, I had a pleasant day in Namche Bazar starting with a thorough wash in a bucket of warm water and shaving off my itchy beard. After dressing in clean underwear I went to the Indian check-post to have my hair cut by their mess orderly. Meanwhile Chowang and Sona washed clothes, and spread them out in the sun. It was good to feel clean and refreshed.

That evening the three Indians from the check-post came to dinner, chicken with local vegetables, chapattis and marmalade and rich fruit cake. My liaison officer was quickly in a drunken stupor, explaining, no doubt, why the *raksi* ran out before the meal was over. Anyway, the Indians left expressing gratitude and 'brotherly feelings'. I walked around the village afterwards enjoying a beautiful night with a full moon and snow peaks outlined against a starlit sky. Since there was little to do before the women came down to Namche, I decided to make a brief side-trip to the Everest Base Camp, less than an easy day's march away.

Monday, October 19th: Namche to Thangboche

I slept till 7 a.m. and reluctantly got out of my sleeping bag. After an early lunch Chowang led the way along a path winding above the Milk River through a scene of breathtaking beauty, deciduous trees among the firs and pines on wooded slopes below, moorland heather above, and Everest and Ama Dablam and other high peaks against the skyline. It was a lovely sunny day with hardly a cloud. After several hours the track dropped to a wooden bridge where the river was spouted by boulders into a huge gush of natural power that showered us with spray as we crossed.

Beyond it were four squat temples just big enough to cover huge prayer wheels, and then the path followed a crystal-clear stream until we climbed steeply through lovely woodlands. Here we met the

Lama of Khumjung who was returning home after a visit to Thangboche monastery at the foot of Everest, where we hoped to spend the night. Clouds made their usual evening rise to hide Everest and the other peaks as we climbed for an hour from the river up a steep track to the monastery. This holy place was huge and grubby, but Chowang found us lodgings in the *gumba* (private prayer house) of one of the 30 Lamas. Our host sat in the courtyard, patching richly coloured robes for a festival due shortly. His house was the cleanest I'd seen in Nepal, but the red robes he wore were filthy.

He had a picture of his sister with her husband and child who live in Kalimpong on a sort of dressing table, and a picture of an Indian girl in a soap advert stuck to the wall. I was astonished to find he also had a copy of the previous February 8th's *Women's Daily Mirror*, which could only have been left by Mrs Morin, the woman who figured as the heroine of a story I had written about an ill-fated Ama Dablam expedition. It was strange to see adverts for Billy Butlin's holiday camp and other things that seemed so unreal in that place.

The Lama made us Tibetan tea using ghee and salt instead of milk and sugar. When it was mashed he poured it into a thin 3-foot high dolly tub made of wood in brass rings and gave it a good pounding before putting it back in the kettle to serve it in china cups on silver stands. Chowang cooked supper on a fire in the courtyard and the Lama joined us for dinner of canned Irish stew, rice, potato and a green vegetable like cabbage. The Lama smiled happily as he tasted tinned rice pudding. I logged the meal as 'very good'.

During the meal Ratna talked about politics and democracy, and I was surprised to find his limited vocabulary was more suited to that than to translating information from Chowang. In a night of glorious starlight with peaks of Everest, Ama Dablam and Lhotse, ghostly-looking, shrouded in mist, was a scene of indescribable, breathless beauty, a tinsled wonderland. As I stood alone, the banging of the monastery drums made it all the more eerie. The last thing I heard before sleeping was the sound of prayers chanted by the Lama.

Tuesday, October 20th: Thangboche to Namche

I was awakened by the Lama chanting prayers again, got up

quickly and found Chowang on the terrace already busy with the cooking fire. We had tea, boiled eggs and hard biscuits. It was another beautiful clear day with Everest and the other peaks glistening in sunlight, although we had to wait till 8 a.m. before it was high enough to warm the valley. As the first rays touched the monastery walls there was a banging of gongs, and a blaring of trumpets from a temple tower and loud chanting.

Views from that monastery must be unrivalled. Beside it was a wide saddle of turf, edged by pretty groups of trees and rhododendrons, with more fine woodland thickets dotting a grass ridge sloping down to the moraine valley from Everest where the stream trickling down from Everest grows quickly and becomes the Milk River. Stabbing the sky like towering guardian towers on all sides are the world's highest snow peaks. We climbed the four easy miles to the rubbish-strewn site of the Everest Base Camp, no eye-catching place in itself, then headed down the stream that grew into the Milk River.

Chowang began prancing around like an ape with a devilish grin on his face. I realised he wanted to say something about the Yeti, the so-called Abominable Snowman of legend. I had often quizzed the Sherpas about this legendary man-like animal, and been told that it really did exist and sometimes carried off Sherpa women as mates. Ratna said Chowang wanted to detour to a village called Pangboche to see a relic of a dead Yeti in the temple there, and I remembered reading about the discovery of a Yeti scalp in a temple near Everest. When we reached the tiny temple there, a shabby Lama opened a cupboard door and produced from an assortment of masks and adornments used at festivals a strange sort of skull cap. It was partly covered with bristly hairs about three inches long in a blend of reddish brown and almost black-brown. It was evidently used as a skull cap for a dancer in the masked dances sometimes held in the temple courtyard. There was no stitching in the tough skin so its shape was natural enough.

Ratna, helping out his language frustration with signs, indicated that it had been cut from the head of a Yeti in a circle above the ears, and it was several hundred years old. He said I could take away a few of the hairs if I made a further contribution of 100 rupees to temple funds, but I declined the offer.

However, I became less sceptical about the Yeti when I learned that Dannu, the women's cook Sherpa, had told Chowang how a friend of his had been attacked by a Yeti while crossing Nagpa La Pass, and so severely mauled that he died. I was half inclined to climb back to the monastery and pay 100 rupees for Yeti hairs. I resisted that fancy and we continued on to Namche in what I logged as 'one of the most beautiful walks in the world'.

The Nepalese Major met us as we entered Namche just after midday, and invited me to lunch. After a quick shave at my lodgings I joined Margaret Darvall, Loulou Boulaz, and the women's liaison officer, Mr Sharma, around the Major's table. What a treat it was – partridge shot on the hillside above, curried rice, curds and chapatti. Over it, the women and I swapped yarns about Thangboche, which they had visited a few days before. They had taken a tent with them as women were not allowed to sleep in the monastery. After two hours' bargaining in the afternoon, I bought a Tibetan apron for 20 rupees and the Tibetan rug I saw being made by my landlady for 80 rupees.

That night there was talk in the bazaar that the women had reached Thami and would be arriving next day, a day earlier than I had calculated. I planned to see them through Namche Bazar and then hurry back to Kathmandu ahead of them, as I was anxious to be in direct cable touch with my office. I still had no idea how my cables were landing and how they had been used.

PART TWO

THE WOMEN'S STORY

Chapter Seven

Avalanche

Claudine and Sherpas Wangdi and Ang Norbu had established Camp Four on September 29th. It nestled in a slight hollow at the bottom of the final summit slopes, apparently safely distant from the edge of ice cliffs with a sheer drop of thousands of feet into a deep crevasse on the northern side of the mountain. At 24,300 feet it was within a half-day's climb of the summit in favourable conditions. They pitched a small tent and left equipment and some food and returned to join Claude Kogan at Camp Three. There Wangdi, the expedition Sirdar and veteran of many expeditions, advised Madame Kogan that the break in the weather was not to be relied upon.

He pressed her as strongly as a paid employee was able to do. He told her that monsoon conditions of sudden change were still around, and the real break in the weather had yet to come. He also advised that present snow conditions were unsuitable – the depth of snow on exposed parts of the mountain provided danger from avalanches.

In the meantime the women at Camp One had made the most of a day of clear sunshine. They dug themselves out of deep snow and busied themselves making up loads. Sherpa Chepala brought Claude Kogan's note from Camp Three saying, 'Claudine has gone up to Camp Four with Nawong and Ang Norbu. Snow is very, very deep. I hope they can make a depot up there. I have sent a note down to Jeanne about future plans. I am sending Chepala back from Camp Three because there is only one tent there. Please send up another tent as soon as possible. There are not enough stores here either. If you have a Sherpa to bring up your bedding come up to Camp Three because without doubt Claudine and I will be going up to Camp Four tomorrow to sleep.

'That will permit us to try for the summit, if the weather is good, on October 2nd. In principle Claudine and I will make the first try for the summit. If we don't succeed then you and Jeanne must try, with Eileen if she is fit. It's impossible to plan further ahead. I want you to come to Camp Three today and do your best to establish it properly.'

In another note to her old friend Jeanne Franco, Claude Kogan admitted her extreme fatigue. She wrote, 'I am at Camp Three. The way up was very hard yesterday. I had to push myself because the snow was so deep. I am weary. Tomorrow I am sleeping at Camp Four. We will try for the summit on October 2nd, but if the weather is not good I shall fall back on Camp Three or even Camp Two.'

On September 29th, her second day back at Base Camp, Eileen Healey noted, 'There is always a problem of accommodation at Camp One so I stayed another night at Base (laziness really). Just before 10 a.m. Pem-Pem set out with Sona to go to Camp One, with Sona going on to Camp Two. Pem-Pem had recieved a note from Claudine suggesting she should go up, and a bad eye she had complained about was better in a moment.[1] Various Sherpas came down, saying how tired they all were, but Claudine apparently never tires and eats like a horse, although Wangdi says the Sherpas can't eat higher up.'

Next day, September 30th, Eileen Healey wrote, 'A rest day at Base. I had intended to go up to Camp One, but if I insisted I knew Wangdi would send a tired Sherpa with me. In the afternoon we saw a figure descending, obviously tired out. It was Phu Dorje. He had descended to Camp One the previous day, tried to return to Camp Two but hadn't made it. He left his load and came down.

'He had a temperature. Wangdi was most annoyed. He said Sherpas had temperatures off and on. He had one himself, but Phu Dorje was needed up top and would have to go back next day. Quite right I suppose. With so many people it must take most of our Sherpa strength to get food to them without pushing to higher camps.'

When Sherpas Darwa Norbu and Chepala returned from Base Camp that day with Pem-Pem and Sherpa Sona they dumped the loads they carried and took on fresh loads containing the most important items needed at the higher camps.

Jeanne Franco went down to Base Camp and Gravina set off for

---

[1] Claudine had written a brief note from Camp Three to Pem-Pem, who had shared her tent during the approach march, saying, 'Come to see us Pem-Pem. It is so beautiful here. I need you to go to the top of Cho Oyu – Claudine.'

Camp Two with Darwa Norbu and Chepala. Gravina found it hard work with the snow deep and soft and the sun baking hot. They passed a party of Sherpas on their way down and paused to exchange news.

She wrote in her diary, 'The going was very bad in spite of the down tracks[2], but we crawled on up. One slid back at every step, a most exhausting and frustrating process. We tumbled thankfully into the hollow of Camp Two (21,600 feet), and ate an enormous supper. Whether it was that or altitude I don't know but both Sherpas complained of headaches in the night and pains here and there, so in the early hours I dug out the most lurid-looking pills I could find which produced a miraculous recovery.'

Both Sherpas went on from Camp Two up to Camp Three with the most urgent supplies, leaving Gravina alone at Camp Two. She noted, 'It was a heavenly day. There was plenty to do, and I spent it happily sorting out loads and clearing up generally.

'Towards sunset I sat perched up on the ridge with all that marvellous view spread out below – to the north, the arid brown of Tibet stretching away to the horizon; to the west, beyond Nangpa La, miles of magnificent great snowy peaks glistening in the sun; and to the south, the jagged icy points and battlements of the main ridge. There was a fierce storm raging over Everest, a seething cauldron of cloud boiling up into the sky, but at Camp Two all was peaceful.'

The cold grew intense after the sun went down. Gravina had a pan of snow melting to prepare supper when she heard shouts from above and below. Pem-Pem and Sona came from below, and Sherpa Chepala from above with the note from Claude Kogan written at Camp Three.

At Base Camp on October 1st, Eileen Healey noted, 'All Sherpas but Phu Dorje with Nima and Douma left at 7.15 a.m. for Camp Two, the girls setting an incredible pace. I decided to set out later. Sky overcast at first, but sun coming through. Wangdi seems pessimistic about the weather, says the monsoon ought to have finished but hasn't and winter is coming and the Sherpas complaining they haven't clothing for cold. Colette returned from Namche with Gyalzen and about eight other Sherpas.

'Clouds getting lower and I should like to set out this morning

---

[2] Broken by the Sherpas they had met.

81

but Jeanne still wants to go this afternoon. We set out with Phu Dorje and settled into Camp One just before Nowung and Darwa Norbu arrived. Nowung stayed with us and Darwa Norbu insisted on continuing to Base, although in his state of tiredness it was criminal of us to let him go alone in the snow.'[3]

The weather changed during that night, and on the morning of October 1st it looked threatening. Gravina and Sona, laden with a tent and stores, set off up the ice cliff. Neither had been to Camp Three before, but they followed marker flags and tracks. Countess Gravina noted in her diary later, 'As we ploughed upwards the weather got worse and it began to snow. We reached a sheltered little hollow protected by a wall of ice at the back and there were a few stores lying around. We decided this couldn't be Camp Three yet so we named it Depot Three.'

Pressing on, they followed faint tracks and flags marking a route to the left, weaving in and out of an area of crevasses, coming out on to the open face of the mountain which swept up almost unbroken to the summit. They could seen no sign of Camp Three. By that time it was snowing hard, visibility was closing in.

Eileen Healey added, 'We didn't like the look of it at all, so we turned back to Depot Three, pitched the tent, anchored it firmly with hefty wooden stakes and stowed all the stores and gear inside, and then went down to Camp Two – surely the top party would do likewise in this weather.

'At Camp Two we found all three girls and a lot of Sherpas. It was a tight fit in the ice cave and two small tents. We were packed like sardines in the cave for supper and as usual when the fug managed to rise to a comfortable degree, the ice roof dripped steadily on to everybody and everything.'

Three Sherpas from Camp Four arrived at Camp Two carrying a series of messages. The first from Claude Kogan, written at Camp Three, seemed irrational in view of the weather, but it explained why they had been unable to find Camp Three.

It said, 'We have decided to go up today to Camp Four. Without doubt we shall establish the camp and take a few steps towards the top. We shall sleep at Camp Four with Ang Norbu. Camp Three is

---

[3] Dawa Norbu stayed in bed for four days worn out with many days at high altitude. He had carried a message from Ang Norbu to Wangdi saying that Camp Four was a very dangerous place and said he needed help to come up as soon as possible.

non-existent because we have brought the tent up here. You must come up to Camp Three with all the Sherpas you can and establish it. Bring two tents and make an ice house. It is essential that Camp Three and Camp Four should be firmly established. Tomorrow you must send up one Sherpa with Wangdi to help us.'

In a note written on the back of this message, Claudine van der Stratten explained why they had taken the only tent from Camp Three, thus cutting off a vital refuge in their line of retreat. She wrote, 'We go to Camp Four. We are not quite sure whether Sherpas from Camp Two will arrive in time, so can't count on them to make us a grotto, so we are taking the tent from Camp Three. We will send you a note this evening giving more exact planning according to conditions we find up there.'

At 1.30 p.m. on September 30th Claude Kogan wrote the last note she was able to send down the mountain with returning Sherpas. It was written at Camp Four, 24,300 feet up, 2,450 feet below the summit, a matter of 150 feet or so below the point at which a man's decision had forced Madame Kogan to turn back in 1954.

It said, 'Bad weather, but safe with everything necessary to hold out. We are very tired. Having remade the track, put up the tent, the Sherpas are tired out. We are sending three of them back and keeping Ang Norbu. Tomorrow we shall stay in our sleeping bags and rest. You must establish Camp Three and send up Wangdi and a strong Sherpa.'

A blizzard raged all night with wind gusts of up to 100 mph and Gravina called Wangdi to her tent to consider what might be done to rescue the three people high above them. It was clearly a time to forget the women's attitude that they were able to do anything a man could do.

Gravina wrote 'We were both uneasy but at that time neither of us thought seriously of avalanches on the upper route. His plan was to go up to Camp Four as rapidly as possible and hurry them down as the weather shows no sign of improving. It seemed the best thing to do though I didn't like it much. His answer was invariably "It is my duty." I wrote a note to Claude and at dawn watched Wangdi and Chewang disappear up the ice cliff. It was useless for me to go with them. They would go much faster than I could and speed was important.

'My job was to clear the camp to make room for the top party to move in, and above all to get the three girls down to safety as rapidly as possible. Wangdi was keen to have all camps cleared to Base so that the five above Camp Two could move down very quickly.'

At dawn on October 2nd Wangi set off back up the mountain with Sherpa Chewang. Some of the women tried to stop him, saying it was not safe. Wangdi replied, 'It is my duty', and went on fastening his crampons.

Snow was falling as the women watched the two men disappear into a white blur. Later these last occupants of Camp Two struggled down the mountain through deep snow. Just above Camp One a small avalanche slid past them.

Gravina noted, 'My unease turned to grave anxiety. It had turned noticeably warmer. There could be no going back.'

At Camp One they shed crampons as usual for the last part of the descent, and also their high-altitude reindeer boots, and continued in ordinary climbing boots. Jeanne and Eileen, the occupants of Camp One, joined the party for the last stage, amid the thunder of avalanches sweeping the mountain in all directions.

Eileen Healey wrote this in her diary that day: 'Snowed all night and very warm, continued snowing today. Stayed in tents mostly until there was a cry that all at Camp Two were on their way down. Many avalanches were coming down and we were thankful when they arrived safely. Lapka had broken the trail with Dorothea at the end of the first rope ready to belay in case of emergency. The girls on the second rope were well Sherpa'd but seemed to need little encouragement to get down. Dorothea said that Claude and Claudine and Ang Norbu were at Camp Four and Wangdi and Chewang were to bring them down. I was rather horrified at the thought of no support at any of the camps, but they were well provisioned and it was a strong party on top. Also what could I do? I was incapable of going to Camp Two in that snow and I considered it too dangerous to stay at Camp One since the largest avalanche had covered the tents in spray.'

At 7 p.m., as Gravina and Eileen Healey shared a guttering candle to write their diary accounts, they heard a faint call and leapt out, calling to the Sherpas clustered around the fire in the kitchen shelter. The Sherpas rushed out into the driving snow with lamps and a kettle of tea, and found Wangdi crawling along in the last stages of exhaustion. All he could say was 'Chewang is dead.'

84

Tensing with Eileen Healey and Claudine van der Straten.

Madame Kogan,
Countess Gravina and
Tensing.

Pause to type the story of the loss of Madame Kogan and Claudine van der Straten after meeting runners from Base Camp.

Typing notes at the women's Base Camp. Countess Gravina and Madame Jeanne Franco with me, reading from their diaries.

With Chowang
inside Tibet.

Author taking a
rest at 20,000
feet, one mile
inside Tibet.

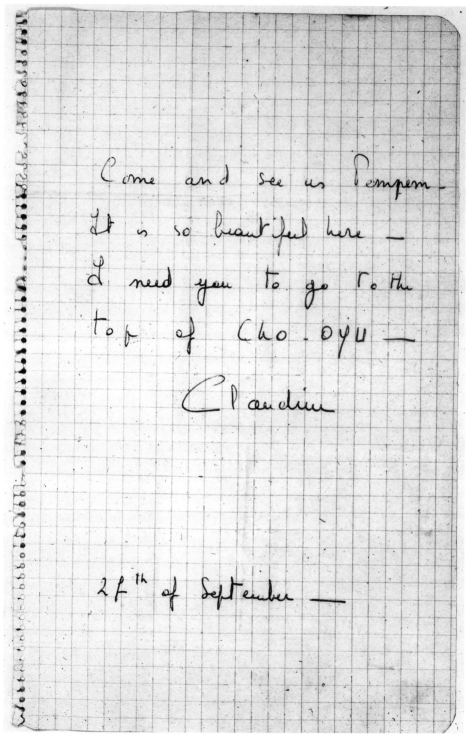

Note written by Claudine van der Straten from Camp Four, just before her death. It was written to Pem-Pem Norhay, daughter of Tensing.

Loulou Boulaz and Margaret Darvall with their Namche Bazar landlady.

The author breakfasting with the expedition at Base Camp.

First view of the women's Base Camp from the Tibetan side.

Countess Gravina and Eileen Healey took me above 21,000 feet to get the best view of Cho Oyu.

The author and Countess Gravina at nearly 20,000 feet on a neighbouring Tibetan peak.

Countess Gravina with Sherpa Wangdi, hands bandaged because of frostbite.

The *Sunday Express* splashed the first full account of the tragic end of the all-woman expedition.

They wrapped him in blankets and carried him to the kitchen shelter where as Dr le Bret tended his frostbitten hands he gasped out a story of an avalanche that overwhelmed him and Chewang.

He said he and Chewang had just got above Camp Three (23,000 feet) and could see three flags ahead of them. Chewang was leading and when Wangdi fell over in what felt like an earthquake Chewang shouted to him to hurry because of the danger of avalanches where they were. Then an avalanche started under their feet and swept them both down. Wangdi had cut his way out of the snow in a struggle lasting about two hours. He had tried to free Chewang, but he was buried too deep. He cut the rope, and struggled down to Base Camp.

From his pockets they recovered the note Countess Gravina had written to Madame Kogan that morning. It is a telling document, almost mutinous in telling an expedition leader that she was to be brought down to Base Camp to make a better plan. It was datelined October 2nd, Camp 2, and read: 'Dear Claude, What weather! This morning Wangdi is going up to Camp Four to bring you back to Base Camp, which seems the best thing to do. Everybody else is going down. He said this weather may continue for days, and that no purpose is being served sitting up in the air eating everything that has been carried up. Also the Sherpas are tired, and that would give them a rest. I hope you agree. It seems to me that it will help a good deal to start again with a good plan.

'Also I'm sure it is not good for Claudine's health to stay so long at such altitude. These are my thoughts but I'm quite sure you will have some others. I am quite ready to consolidate Camp Three but it serves no purpose while it is snowing hard. Dorothea.'

The roar of avalanches went on all that night, and Gravina noted in her diary, 'There could be no question of going up in those conditions. The worst part was our helplessness. There was nothing we could do: either they were in safety as Claude had said, or else they were already beyond help.'

Later that evening Eileen Healey returned to her diary to write, 'Wangdi had been able to put his hand across his face and give himself a little air to breathe and gradually enlarge the space with his hand until he could reach his penknife. He cut his hand but also managed to cut himself free of the rope and rucksack and get out. He shouted and searched for Chewang without success. Then he struggled down alone and managed to call twice, but hadn't strength left to call any more. Pem-Pem translated when he murmured "Chewang is dead" – Chewang the one with the greatest sense of humour, always laughing and apparently leaving two small children and elderly parents.'

Days of anxious waiting followed until conditions on the mountain became less dangerous and a search for their lost companions could begin. Blizzards whipped, shrieked and howled around the tents and rock shelters of Base Camp throughout October 3rd, piling snow higher and higher. Shattering roars echoed around the cliff faces as avalanches ripped the sides of the mountain apart. Immense weights of snow, lodged high up on Cho Oyu under the pressure of 125 mph winds, became too heavy to hold and crashed downwards in swirling white fury that nothing could withstand. For anyone to have survived would need a miracle, and it was for that miracle that the women at Base Camp prayed.

At Namche Bazar, which I had reached the day before, I noted, 'Rain has fallen for 36 hours without cease, and the snow-line has crept down to a few hundred feet above us. Must be rough in the mountains.'

At Base Camp Eileen Healey recorded, 'Gylatzen and Sona went up to the rock col. The traverse at the top had become too dangerous with the mass of snow. They shouted across but got no answer.

'Because of the mist they were unable to see Camps Three and Four, but Camp One appeared all right though there had been avalances on both sides. In the afternoon Wangdi was able to sit up and talk to us.'

Next day she noted, 'It was colder in the night, and I hoped that indicated a change of weather, but the morning clouded over. Dorothea and four Sherpas went up to the col and spent the day there to watch for signs of life and anyone descending. Jeanne and Colette joined them. Wangdi talks of getting up the mountain again, but his hands are badly blistered and warmth has not returned to all his fingers.'

On October 5th she wrote, 'We thought of keeping quiet about the loss of those at Camp Four, but realised rumours would go round Ang Norbu's village. Decided to send telegrams about them being lost in a storm and all hope abandoned for Margaret and Loulou by wireless to Colonel Roberts. Also decided Ang Norbu's widow would have to be told.'

The first break in the weather came that day, clearing sufficiently for Countess Gravina to go up to the col with two Sherpas. For the first time on this first section of the climb she roped up with Sherpas to cross the gullies, some having avalanched and the others remaining unstable. They could see the whole mountain and searched it with glasses for two hours.

Gravina noted 'Hoping against hope to see some sign of movement, but there was absolutely nothing. The whole face of the mountain had avalanched. Camp One was intact with avalanches all around it. The snow was in very dangerous condition.'

On the morning of October 6th, she noted, 'Woke up with a terrible sense of burden. The full tragedy of the situation broke over me, but one cannot brood on these things. There is too much to do. Wangdi wants his Sherpas to rush up to Camp Four. I agree on clear understanding there are no risks. We just cannot have more accidents.'

Later that morning she judged the snow movement had settled down enough to begin the quest to find out the fate of the two women and Sherpa Ang Norbu. She and Eileen Healey led two Sherpas, who carried their sleeping bags and provisions, up the mountain in proper expedition style. The going was hard in deep snow, and they had a long search to find Camp One among huge mounds of piled-up snow. Clouds came up from the valleys covering the slopes in thick mist. Eventually what appeared to be a snow-covered box turned out to be a buried tent.

Night came down at 4 p.m. and they spent 15 hours of intermittent sleep huddled in sleeping bags. Gravina noted, 'It was all a nightmare.'

Eileen Healey gave that day this brief note: 'Dorothea and I had early lunch before starting up at noon, reached Camp One and shovelled snow out of the tents. Jeanne and Colette arrived later with Sherpas Lakpa and Chepala. Good weather. Good snow.'

Camp One was in a hollow, missing out on the caressing warmth of the sun that quickly turns the fearsome long mountain nights into a totally different world, a scenic wonderland. Mountain shadow breeds lassitude, demanding the greatest effort of will to move or do anything. But unpleasant though it was, Camp One was well sited. It remained undisturbed by any of the trails of avalanches scarring the snow slopes all around.

As the women were breakfasting on October 7th, Sherpa Gombu

passed with three Sherpas, accompanied by Jeanne Franco and Colette le Bret. Gombu and the Sherpas carried on immediately towards Camp Two and the women followed in their trail later. Countess Gravina noted, 'The going was terrible – steep soft snow all the way. Snow accumulated like a ball under our crampons making feet already burdened with high-altitude boots and crampons dead weights.'

The sun was hot, and the only relief was that the Sherpas had broken the trail ahead. All of them, women and Sherpas alike, were exhausted when they reached Camp Two. The four women shared two small tents and the five Sherpas slept in the ice cave. The inside of the ice cave was an untidy mess of bedding, gas cooking stoves and stores, but the four women joined the Sherpas for supper inside the igloo-style doorway where there was just room to sit up. As the cave warmed up water dripped from the roof.

After eating they shared the remains of a bottle of whisky, running to a tot each. Eileen Healey described it as 'too sordid for words', but Countess Gravina noted, 'I had mine with hot toddy. It was wonderful, but it seemed very sad not to be toasting the summit. It was very cold. We put on every garment we could find to go to bed.'

The Sherpas were astir early next morning, October 8th, for Gombu, anxious to see what conditions were like higher up, had diplomatically taken his own decision to act while the women were still asleep. Countess Gravina left her sleeping bag just in time to see the four Sherpas leave, and noted in her diary, 'I couldn't have them go off into the cold without any of the Memsahibs up to see them off.'

The four expedition women followed later, intending that Countess Gravina and Jeanne Franco should sleep at Depot Three and the others return to Camp Two. Following the trail broken by the Sherpas they came to the trickiest stretch of the entire route up the mountain, a nerve-testing ascent of ice cliffs with a 2,000 foot-drop beneath. They reached the snow slopes above this trickiest stretch only to find the Sherpas coming down.

Gombu reported that they had reached the location of Camp Three without finding any sign of it. They had found Wangdi's rucksack and rope in one avalanche, He had been carried 75 feet down the mountain from the marked trail. Gombu said that conditions were still too dangerous higher up for any attempt to reach the site of Camp Four.

As they talked they saw a lone figure climbing towards them. It was Sherpa Gylazen, who had left Base Camp that morning with mail from home, the most recent dated five weeks before. He also carried bananas and peaches from the tropical valleys below Namche Bazar. After enjoying this fresh fruit picnic sitting on the snow slope, they all returned to Camp Two for a second uncomfortable night.

On October 9th it was decided to wait another day for snow conditions to stabilise. Eileen Healey noted, 'Rest day so we didn't stir until long after the sun had reached our tent. The Sherpas said they were willing to try again next day, but that didn't suit Dorothea and Jeanne who wanted to move up to Camp Three before the attempt, so it was put off for another day.'

Every one of the Sherpas complained of ailments, and all were exhausted. Morale was low, but spirits rose when Countess Gravina announced definite plans for the next day. Dr le Bret was to return to Base Camp where she was needed to check Wangdi's hands and change the dressing, and the rest of them would make a recce to Camp Four. They passed the day instructing the Sherpas how to operate cameras so that they could not only salvage such papers and belongings as they might find, but also photograph the scene where Camp Four had been. This was another admission by these tough, resolute women that the Sherpas were likely to climb higher than they might be able to, not perhaps because they were male, but because they were in their own environment.

Light snow was falling and it was bitingly cold on the morning of October 10th. The Sherpas set out, but the sight of a Sherpa messenger heading up to them from Base Camp delayed the women's departure. He carried my message written to Countess Gravina on October 8th, expressing frustration that runners from Base Camp I had met three days above Namche told me that they had instructions to give messages to nobody but the Memsahibs at Namche, forcing me to go all the way down to Namche to collect them. Countess Gravina immediately dashed off a four-page note and sent it back down the mountain for forwarding on to me.

So it was already afternoon when she, Jeanne Franco and Sherpa Phu Dorje struggled up to Depot Three, floundering through deep snow, summoning the last dregs of effort. In a later note to me, dated Base Camp on October 12th, Countess Gravina described how tricky the passage up the ice cliffs was in deep snow although safeguarded by ropes: 'One goes up a steep slope to a big ice overhang, then a little traverse under the ice bulge, then up another very steep slope to a good foot-hold on the lip of a crevasse – above the slope is a sheer wall of ice and snow, below you can shoot down gaily 2,000 feet non-stop. Then comes the tricky bit: a few feet of really chancy footsteps, the ice wall on the left and if you don't step very close the outer bit of the step is likely to give way – the rope along here was always pretty loose, I never knew why, but anyway one held on to it jolly hard. Then up an airy bit into space and so gradually up a steep slope to safety.'

She added, 'We went on up to Depot Three where Sona and I had pitched a tent on October 1st when the weather broke on our way to Camp Three. It was intact, only iced up a bit, no avalanches. It had been the most painful jaunt I have ever done. Each leg seemed like a lump of lead. I was puffing and panting so much I thought I would never make it. It took every ounce of will-power to get there, inch by inch. My worst day. I flopped thank-fully down by the tent when at last we made it. We spent the night lying sardine fashion just able to get our three airbeds in the tiny tent. The cold was perishing.

'In the morning (October 11th) it took me half-hour to thaw my reindeer boots enough to get into them. Outside the cold wind nearly froze off one's nose. Three strong Sherpas came up from Camp Two (where they had gone down for the night) and went on to Camp Four with instructions to take photographs, etc just in case we couldn't make it.

'We followed on, found Camp Three completely vanished, swept clean by avalanches. Also the rope leading to Chewang. He had obviously gone down deep under the avalanche. I cut away the rope. We went on towards Camp Four, right up to the great open face of the mountain. Avalanches had poured down everywhere. The snow was still very deep with an ice crust on top, and I must admit I was thankful to get off the snow slopes. We came up to just below the top band of rock which runs across the mountain below the summit. There is a hollow there, full of crevasses. Camp Four had been pitched just above the rocks – not a sign of it or anything, the whole area had been swept clean as a whistle. One can only suppose that tent and occupants were overwhelmed and swept down a crevasse when the whole face avalanched.

'It is wonderful up there, great majestic mountains in all directions, miles of Tibet below. I have no words to describe the beauty of it. They could not have found a finer resting place, so near the summit their hearts longed for. The tragedy is not for them. They are where they chose to be. The tragedy is for those left, the two Sherpa families with young children, the parents and friends in Europe.'

Sadly, in a bitter wind that seemed to penetrate their layers of padded clothing, they slithered and stumbled down the mountain, pausing to strike the single tent at Depot Three, to Camp Two where Eileen Healey and Gravina overnighted while the others went on down to Base Camp.

During the planning stage of the expedition Countess Gravina, a grandmother, had doubted whether she would be able to make Base Camp, barely more than 19,000 feet. That day she had reached almost as high – short by less than 1,000 feet – as the altitude that gained Claude Kogan the women's record.

Among Madame Kogan's last notes was this comment: 'It is interesting to see how people's ambitions grow with physical form. Dorothea, the eldest, had at the beginning only the ambition to get to Base Camp. But once she had been to Camp One she wanted to get to Camp Two. There she built a very good ice cave and she is talking already of going up to Camp Three. I hope with all my heart that she will be able to make 23,000 feet.'

In her diary that day, Eileen Healey mentioned the note of complaint I had sent to Countess Gravina, adding, 'He had met our postmen at Lunak and they refused to give him letters before Namche. So he had to double march back – I could hardly blame him! We didn't know he had left Kathmandu until our postmen said they had met him Jumbesi way. Dorothea sent a long letter in reply and then set out. I helped Phu Dorje by carrying half his load up to the fixed ropes.'

On October 11th she noted, 'I hadn't slept at all well with wind shaking the tent all night. I only looked out of my sleeping bag as the Sherpas left, and it looked a horrible day. There was nothing I could do. I should have been such a drag on them if I tried to share their hardship.' Tidying camp, she put sleeping bags out to air, and two of them were blown upwards towards the ropes. She ran after them but deep snow slowed her up and they finally disappeared over a ridge.

She continued, 'When Sherpas returned they said the loss of the bags didn't matter as they were going down to Base. They had found Camp Three depot okay, but the site of Camp Three was completely covered by an avalanche. Phu Dorje had stayed at Camp Three but the others had gone on and found Wangdi's sack and the end of the rope, but Chewang was much further down in the avalanche and it would have been impossible to do anything for him. This time the Sherpas had reached Camp Four but found no trace of a tent. The whole site had been swept by an avalanche.

'They said Dorothea, Jeanne and Phu Dorje were still on their way up. After a meal they continued down to Base Camp, promising to return next day. The others came down at about 4 p.m. At 4.30 p.m. Jeanne said she would go down to Base Camp and looked at Phu Dorje who was only too willing to accompany her. Dorothea and I said we'd stay to see to the evacuation of the camp next day. Dorothea and Jeanne were very pleased with themselves having got to almost 6,400 metres, an unusual height for women.'

These last two women on the mountain found the remains of a bottle of whisky among the stores, just enough to take a nip each after cooking supper.

Next morning, October 12th, the remaining tents at Camp Two were struck and so were those at Camp One on their way down. Back at Base Camp Eileen Healey noted, 'When the Sherpas arrived at Camp Two they threw out a lot of food we had packed, saying they could carry only one box. It was a perfect day, but I found the going most exhausting. We paused at Camp One for drinks, and were met at Base Camp by Dannu with tea.'

The mountain was left to the dead.

Chapter Eight

Sadness and a Party in Namche Bazar

During the last days at Base Camp the women mounted a brass and teak memorial on the rock mound which marked where the Indian climber had died of pneumonia at Base Camp a year earlier. They also left a tin memorial made from old kerosene cans with 'Claude Kogan and Claudine van der Stratten, 1959' scratched on it. They were expected to reach Namche Bazar on Wednesday, October 21st.

Low clouds shut out the otherwise magnificent views as I and my team set out at 10 a.m. to meet them, taking the trail up the Bhote Kosi river towards Cho Oyu for the third time.

Just a few miles above Namche Bazar we met Margaret Darvall, Loulou Boulaz and their liaison officer Sharma on their way back. They had set out early, expecting to meet expedition members on the trail, but had turned back short of Thami. When we reached Thami we found the expedition cook, Dannu, setting up his kitchen in a village house. I typed with the typewriter on my knees on the monastery steps while Chowang and Sona made lunch of tea, boiled eggs and cheese. We had just finished eating when a heavy drizzle began, and soon afterwards word that the Memsahibs were coming brought the whole village out to see them. They presented a colourful pageant in their Red Riding Hood plastic capes, and all seemed well and cheerful as they set up camp for the night.

Countess Gravina was cool towards me, telling me blithely that, despite my warnings, she had accepted Peter Byrne's word that he was not writing for a newspaper. I had asked for photographs of the rough memorial to the two dead expedition members to be taken for the *Express*, and Eileen Healey seemed most reluctant to confirm that they had indeed mounted the memorial on a pile of rocks close by another pile of rocks which the Sherpas called a *chorten* to the memory of their two dead comrades.[1]

---

[1] Only in recent years have I learned from Eileen Healey's diary that Peter Byrne had taken pictures with Michelin's camera so that all the surviving expedition women could be in it, also snapping for himself and the *Daily Mail*!

Despite regret expressed by some of the other women that I was not camping overnight and trekking down with them next day, I decided to return to Namche Bazar. We reached my lodgings just before dusk, soaked through but able to change into dry clothes immediately.

I had supper with the two resident Memsahibs in Gyalzen's house, and went back to a second supper which Chowang had already prepared. I made this entry in my log: 'Drank *raksi* rather too indulgently, and sang in bed for an hour to the intense amusement of the household.'

Added to my worry about what Countess Gravina might have told Peter Byrne was the discovery that my last package of compo rations, supposed to contain ten days' supply, contained only enough for three days. Noting this in my diary, I added, 'Just as well I have grown used to Sherpa food.'

Next day, Thursday, October 22nd, rain came down in torrents all day, and I felt sorry for the women on the trail above as I stayed in the warmth of my lodgings until the expedition had had time to settle into their camp on the ridge above Namche Bazar. When I called on them, Countess Gravina revealed the reason for her coolness at Thami. She bawled me out for borrowing a note which Claudine had sent down from Camp Four to Pem-Pem Tenzing. I pointed out that Pem-Pem had been quite willing, even keen, to loan me the note for publication, and that borrowing it was part of my job as a journalist. She responded, 'God help you'. Apparently she saw a world of ethical difference between keeping Captain Scott's diaries in a museum case open for people to read, and reproducing the last note of a woman climber for newspaper readers to see.

The women's return to Namche Bazar was a tears and joy occasion. In the last hamlet before Namche they called at the house of Ang Norbu, one of the missing Sherpas. Eileen Healey noted in her diary, 'The house was neat and tidy and looked reasonably prosperous. Chang and Tibetan tea were served with potato bread. Eventually Mrs Ang Norbu came; what a weeping and gnashing of teeth. No one was able to comfort her, but when Pem-Pem arrived she embraced her.

'Wangdi had to do all the talking, and eventually money was called for, 250 rupees for the poor man's final wages of 37½ pence, then 350 rupees from the seven of us. I felt that was some comfort.

At long last we were able to go on, and just above Namche we were met by the Major with Dorothy and Loulou.'[2]

The women had promised to photograph the memorials for me as their final act at Base Camp, but when I asked for the roll of film there were objections, mainly from the French. Michelin and Jeanne argued that they were private, intended for the relatives and it would be unkind to publish them before the relatives had seen them. They debated it over bowls of tea for so long, with much moralising in rapid French, that I left them to it and joined the Tenzing girls at the check-post where they were listening to songs on All India Radio. Pem-Pem told me she was sorry Countess Gravina had kicked up such a fuss over the note, which she had no doubt the *Express* would return safely to her as I had promised. (They did.)

Later Michelin handed me a roll of film explaining that Jeanne had suggested that I should pretend I had taken the pictures myself, and send notes with prints to the relatives and also make sure Michelin got the negatives back.

Just after dark, as I was slithering through the muddy lanes by torchlight to go to a party at the home of Dannu, the expedition cook, I was hailed by a figure crossing the potato fields. It was Palden, my runner who had left for Kathmandu just 12 days before. He was back with mail that included several telegram cables from the *Daily Express*.

He told me proudly that he had taken just five days to get my urgent message to Kathmandu, the same time as he had taken to carry news of the climbing of Everest to Kathmandu six years before. He had rested a couple of days in Kathmandu before returning. The cables from my office bucked me up as I felt sure that the full story, sent with expedition runners just three hours behind him, must have landed before the news could have broken any other way.

Palden had also brought mail for the women, and this was met with squeals of joy when I took it with me to Dannu's party. It was a good party, and after reading the cables from the *Express* I was in the mood to enjoy it. Everybody was there, men, women and

[2] Widow Norbu and the relatives of Chewang were also told that 2,000 rupees (about £100) would be sent from Kathmandu to both families. This was the government-prescribed compensation for the death of a high-altitude Sherpa, and represented a fortune in Sherpa terms.

children, even babes in arms. The large one-room home above yak stalls was crowded with pressing, mostly unwashed bodies. Bowls of *chockpa*, a Sherpa luxury dish of rice, yak meat, vegetables and chilli, were handed around and eaten on this smart occasion with plastic chopsticks instead of fingers. Two giant butts of *chang* stood on each side for guests to help themselves, and Sherpa ladies in bright rainbow-coloured Tibetan aprons pressed red *raksi*, the local champagne, on those whose glasses were not full.

Sherpa Wangdi, his hands still bandaged, sat by the cooking fire, fed by the French-speaking women, with heavy competition from local women who elbowed them aside to hold brimming bowls of *chang* to the embarrassed Wangdi's lips. Countess Gravina, who had three grown-up sons, cuddled a Sherpa child on her knees, and made me finish her glass of red *raksi*. Eileen Healey, a bride of just over a year, read letters Palden had brought from her husband in Tonbridge.

The Sherpas threw away their cares and danced in Lambeth Walk formation singing low chants to accompany their backwards-shuffling steps. The lines were broken as Sherpa ladies pressed bowls of *chang* to the lips of male dancers, and the floor was soon swimming in creamy *chang*. A few of the expedition women and I attempted to join in with something more like the Lambeth Walk. Chowang watched my intake of liquor anxiously, and warned me the party would last all night. But the European women, used to a seven o'clock bedtime, retired about 8 p.m., and soon afterwards the party broke up in some confusion. I gathered the community were disappointed that the women didn't stick it out till dawn as men of returning expeditions were wont to do.

The following day I left Namche Bazar for the last time, eager to get back to Kathmandu. My diary entry that day, Friday, October 23rd, records, 'Managed to face a huge breakfast of grilled yak steak, got runners away with my despatches by 10 a.m., but many good-byes delayed my own departure till 11.30 a.m.'

Chapter Nine

The Dream Assignment Ends

I set up a record for a non-Sherpa runner in making the return journey from Namche Bazar to Katmandu in eight days, half the recognised light trekking time.

Friday, October 23rd: Namche Bazar to Tate

The porters set out long before I had completed my goodbyes, but after ten minutes down the trail I was surprised to find them resting. It was a sunny day and the scenery was magnificent as Chowang, Ratna and I went rapidly along the Milk River, passing our outward last camp of Juphede at 2 p.m. and pausing for lunch soon afterwards. It was wonderful to be on the way back to normal life and comfort after the weeks of effort, hardship and loneliness.

I made Tate, two days' expedition march, in daylight but the porters, who had wanted to camp since the lunch stop, were lagging, and I lodged in what my log describes as 'the last house before Jumbesi'. The household *chang* was good, but supper was sparse with only processed cheese to go with boiled rice, potatoes and the usual bitter-tasting green cabbage. I slept in the one room with the family and my entire caravan, and the snoring was dreadful. Family chanting of prayers woke us up at dawn.

Saturday, October 24th: Tate to Lejuba

Just boiled eggs and a little raspberry jam for breakfast, and on the way at 7.30 a.m. We took just an hour to reach the top of the first of a series of high ridges before Jumbesi, and I looked back at the Milk River and the Everest group of snow peaks for the last time. It was a lovely, sunny day, but the snow peaks soon became hidden as we crossed mossy, forested ridges.

We pressed on for four hours up a ridge which on our trek to

Namche Ratna had described as 'Our Everest' and down through an alluvial valley, torn by many landslides, looking for a place with firewood to camp. I had treated the porters' demands to camp in the early afternoon as though I thought they were joking, but now it was getting worryingly late. Ratna said we could chip enough wood from a bridge ahead to make a cooking fire, but when we reached it, it was made of rock.

Beyond the next ridge Chowang found a shepherd's shelter, and the occupant was prepared to sell firewood. Our tents were pitched on gravel nearby. We were just an hour short of Sakari Pati. I crawled through the low entrance to the shepherd's shelter in response to an invitation for tea, and was surprised to find the shepherd was a young girl, quite pretty and much bangled. With her was a cousin from Jumbesi and we made polite conversation through Ratna while we drank Tibetan tea. I could imagine many travellers pausing at her hut, and indeed she knew the names of my runners.

Clouds, which had come down in the early afternoon, lifted for a wonderful mauve-tinged sunset over cloud-filled valleys stretching to infinitely far below. I had a frugal omelette supper crouched by the fire in the shelter of rock piled walls. It was a beautiful starlit night, but bitterly cold.

I was determined to make Jumbesi by the following night, but Chowang advised against taking the short-cut over the high ridges above Phudawa where we had had our baptism of extreme cold on the outward trek. He said this late in the year it would be much colder and under snow. The thought of the razor-sharp ridges in piercing wind and snow convinced me. I spent a sleepless night because my sleeping bag was no longer supplemented by yak rugs, although I had the warm rug made by my Namche landlady beneath it.

Sunday, October 25th: Lejuba to Jumbesi

An hour after setting out along the regular trail through Sakari Pati we met expedition runners, the same men I had chased and given my full story of the tragedy. They brought disastrous news, a cable telling me the *Daily Mail* had carried rumours of two women missing on the mountain the morning my full story reached the office in the afternoon, some ten hours too late for that day's paper, and of all days it had to be a Saturday! I was bitterly disappointed. My hopes of a world scoop had been thwarted, firstly because of the women's lies and prevarication, and secondly by the runners who carried my full story taking two days longer to reach Kathmandu than they should have done. 'Bloody bad luck all round', I noted in my log.

I knew from the totally unsympathetic tone of the cable bringing me this calamitous news, signed by foreign desk assistant Jim Thurman, whom I regarded as a friend, that I was to carry the can. I knew how hard Fleet Street could be. Total success was all that counted. The injustice of this ought to have been apparent by the *Sunday Express* still being able to splash my story across its front page as a 'world exclusive with the first full story of the tragic deaths', and Monday's *Daily Express* splashing Countess Gravina's 'Diary of Death Peak' across the front page, but in the eyes of Fleet Street the *Daily Mail* had pulled off a successful spoiler.

I had anyway expected that a brief message sent over Namche radio informing the Nepal government might be released in a press note giving the facts about the women being missing before either of my pairs of runners arrived. I had aimed at presenting a detailed on-the-spot story and pictures to follow such a brief announcement as soon as possible.

In the event, the women had withheld the information from the Nepal government – in breach of their climbing permit which lays down that the facts of success, failure or accident must be reported to the Nepal government before it goes anywhere else.[1] The runners told me they had taken eight days to reach Kathmandu (compared with Palden's five) because, as one of them said casually, they had gone lame.

After meeting the so-called runners, I found the next ridge the hardest of any I had climbed, and trekked on in sunshine for six hours from snow and ice patches to Alpine scenery and scented meadows in deepest gloom. The sight of Ringmo, a tidy farming community with the biggest fields I saw in Nepal, and neatly fenced as well, made me feel better.

Soon labour troubles gave me other things to think about. The

---

[1] When I reached Kathmandu I heard all sorts of skulduggery had been used to try to thwart me, and I reckoned the expedition runners were got at to cause that delay.

porters had at first called me 'Tiger' in an admiring way, but they soon complained that I was setting too fast a pace, although I had guaranteed they would be paid for the normal number of days plus bonuses. We reached Jumbesi, one of the few places big enough to be marked on the guesswork maps then available, by mid-afternoon. Strangely, the fields and the terraces of houses were deserted except for yaks and dogs. At the house we lodged in on the outward march we found the landlady flat out in the hayloft, signs of drunken sickness splashed on her Tibetan dress. She made a quick recovery and swept the balcony clear of hay, and laid rugs for me to sit on.

The box of compo rations which I had forgotten we had left at the house for our return turned out to be another disappointment, for it contained just five tins of mutton – no soup, no porridge.

Expedition runners arrived with more depressing cables from the *Express* foreign desk, but a thank-you from Drew of the *Sunday Express* for providing their page one splash.

Word swept around the tiny hamlet that the typewriting Sahib had hit town again, and soon I was being back-slapped, rib-tickled and almost choked with *chang* and *raksi* pressed upon me. It seemed the whole town was on a binge, but Chowang found two new porters who asked for 20 rupees advance to buy food for the journey, and on Chowang's advice I paid 10 rupees. The carousing went on long into the night, and several times I was awakened by people pleading with me to join in.

Monday, October 26th: Jumbesi to Chyangma

In the bleary dawn only one of the two new porters turned up, and the others, bleary-eyed and obviously unfit to carry loads anyway, refused to move. They thought they had me at their mercy with far more weight in tents, cooking pots and gear than I and my faithful Chowang, somewhat hung-over, could carry. I sought out the village head man, and found him drinking Tibetan tea in his comparatively stately home. Through Ratna I explained the urgency of my need to get to Kathmandu, with veiled threats of telling my friend the King about affairs in his town. He rapidly brought in five young men from farms, and I paid off the mutinous drunks who had been unsatisfactory from the start.

100

It was a relief to leave the arguing, gesticulating drunks, and get on the way again with only one of the old porters soon after eight o'clock. We travelled fast, taking little more than two hours to reach the 12,000-foot pass out of Sherpaland, the last pass above 10,000 feet on our route. The weather high up was grey and misty, but we descended so rapidly to a river valley that my ears felt as though I had just stepped from an airliner.

In four hours we covered ground that had taken a day and a half on the outward trek. It was very hot, and I wished I had changed out of my cavalry twill knickerbockers. Ratna said, 'Altitude finished, rain.' So it was no surprise when drenching rain came soon afterwards as we walked through dense jungle along a river bank, then across a chain bridge, to take shelter on the porch of a house at Chyangma Phedi, short of the place I had hoped to reach. I had dried a clean vest and socks on the back of my rucksack before the rain came, so I changed out of my wet things and sat in vest, underpants and pullover until the porters arrived when I put on cotton trousers.

We had a nip of Scotch each from the remnants of my one bottle to warm us up after dinner of mutton broth, rice and vegetables. I slept badly because of bugs, and watched torrential rain hammering down 2 feet from my bed on the porch most of the night

Tuesday, October 27th: Chyangma Phedi to Changay

We set out through sodden, steaming jungle and after an hour of misery from leeches we emerged into the first broad valley with trees right up to the rounded tops of the surrounding ridges. There were grasshoppers and scores of colourful flowers. While stopping for *chang* at a house I had lodged in on the way out – the one with a picture of the Queen – I heard a noise I had not heard for weeks, the distant sound of an aeroplane engine. Far to the south I saw an old Dakota, the first mechanical vehicle I had seen in six weeks. Later I heard it was taking a party of tourists to see Everest, but low cloud forced it to the south. Before lunch on the banks of the broad river that flows through Those I stripped for my first real bath for weeks.

It was nice to see shops again, even crude open-fronted shops, as we trudged through the narrow paved streets of Those, also known as Meksin. We bought eight eggs for a rupee and a chicken for 3 rupees and cigarettes for the porters. On the track along the river below the town we met my returning runners with mail and rather friendlier cables from the office. These were runners I had despatched from my highest camp at Lunak, and they had made Kathmandu from there in seven days, earning a large bonus.

We pressed on through drizzle and climbed sharply above the river to Changay, where my sleeping bag was positioned on a porch above a chicken coop. My medical knowledge was in demand from all the porters, who feared malaria at valley altitudes, and I gave them aspirins. I also treated two members of the household who had small cuts which I cleaned, daubed with penicillin, and bandaged.

Chowang chopped off the chicken's head to prepare supper, and the thing fluttered headless around the farmyard for several seconds, an appalling sight. I was hungry enough to eat it, but it was tough and I didn't enjoy the meal a bit. We had a spot of whisky and an Ovaltine sort of drink, and slept well.

Wednesday, October 28th: Changay to Kirantichap

I was awakened by the poultry stored under our beds, and up in time to see a crescent moon and stars just before daybreak. Breakfasted on omelette and chapatti, and we were off by 5.45 a.m., quickly crossing the next ridge and down a slippery descent to yet another river. The trail followed it for many miles, frequently switching from one bank to the other over tree-trunk bridges. I had several bad falls on slippery red clay. Keeping a sharp look out for leeches, I caught several before they sneaked through the eye-holes of my boots.

I washed in the river before leaving it for a sharp climb to the next high ridge, from where we could see the trail ahead which lay over a helter-skelter of lower ridges that would take us two days to cover. We could see all the way to the high moors above Dolalghat, where I planned to make my last night camp before Kathmandu. The country was changing, getting warmer and friendlier with every ridge we crossed. At 10 a.m. we passed Yaksa, where on the outward trek I had camped in pouring rain, under really hot sun, among wheat paddy and water meadows with water buffalo instead of yaks, and many houses and fields, lush with flowers and birds and lots of people along the way.

But there was still no sign of any of the fruit I was craving until we climbed the next steep ridge through pine forest and descended the other side to Kirantichap, where we camped again on a pleasant sward of grass shaded by trees. There we bought a man's entire stock of three dozen bananas and ate them greedily, and I found peanuts in a little shop near where my tent was pitched and scoffed them too. They were uncooked and gave me terrible indigestion. It was dusk when the porters arrived, obviously very weary, and the tents were pitched for only the second time since leaving Namche. It was another lovely starlit night. I found a man willing to leave at 3 a.m. carrying a message to Kathmandu for 20 rupees asking for a Landrover to await us, possibly at Banepa where the hospital was being set up.

Thursday, October 29th: Kirantichap to Risenko

I slept well despite bad tummy pains. Our tents were down before dawn and we were on our way by just after 5.30, crossing the river by a crazy chain-metal bridge, and climbing up through pine woods, remembering how painful coming down that ridge had been six weeks earlier. I dropped a little way behind Chowang for a while as my scoffing of the peanuts was producing loud emissions of wind, a source of great amusement to my companions!

Near the top, where farmland replaced pine forest, there was excited shouting ahead and a jackal dashed across the hillside 30 yards away with a white chicken in its mouth and under pursuit by a posse of dogs, men and children. Carrion crows overhead marked the course of the thief's flight. It was a perfect day with Gaurishankar and neighbouring peaks visible in the distance. It was hard to recall in this smiling countryside the sodden misery of the outward trek through it.

Swinging along past a collection of huts near the top of the ridge I recognised the place as Chitra, where I had treated the ten-year-old girl I had thought was likely to die. The house was shut up, windows barred with split logs, and it seemed I had been right, and my treatment had done no good. Chowang remembered the girl, too, and asked about her. The villager smiled happily in a *namaste* greeting of hands together as in prayer, and said the girl had recovered thanks to the *Burro* [big] *Sahib* and was helping her family working distant fields. I supposed the penicillin would have been more potent with a patient who had never received Western drugs before. I went on my way cheered by that news.

On the narrow track down the other side of that ridge we met more returning runners, and paused soon afterwards for lunch, when I read my mail and was bucked by rather nice telegrams about story usage. Further down we saw our first citrus fruit, lemons and oranges growing in the garden of an empty house. Ratna scrumped some while I bathed in a nearby fast-flowing river.

Further along we came to an orchard and bought three giant bhagya fruits, rather like an overgrown grapefruit with thick skin and deliciously juicy flesh, a large melon and a dozen oranges, all for 1½ rupees. We sat down in the middle of the track to eat them and shared them with the delighted porters as they caught up.

As we approached the monastery at Risenko I saw a tent pitched on the grass banks beside it. Fearing Fleet Street rivals I hurried up the steep climb from yet another river crossing in a final burst of energy that surprised me, as I had been flagging long before we came upon the fruit. As I approached the tent a man reclining on an airbed sprang to his feet and called in strongly accented English, 'Are you Harper?' He introduced himself as Gerard Gery, a photographer for Paris-Match, which had been taking *Express* coverage of the expedition. Greatly relieved that he was not from a rival paper or news agency, I happily joined him for my best meal since the Nepalese Major's lunch at Namche. We had onion soup, tasty meat and sauté potatoes, and tinned fruit salad.

Gery told me he was on his way to meet the women. He had left Geneva at the time I left Namche Bazar and had been three days on the trail. It was good to get into my sleeping bag that night, replete with good food and the latest news of a world that had become a memory. I was also tired out. We had trekked 12 hours that day.

Friday, October 30th: Risenko to Chakhola

Before Gery was astir, I said a brief goodbye to him through his tent doorway and we set out at 6.30 a.m., descending to the next river, following its course for awhile, then up a long, steep climb to an interminable high rhododendron forest before the sun became unbearably hot. The moors beyond seemed just as endless as the forest, but at last we reached the edge of the high plateau, and looked down the thousands of feet of steep hillside to Dolalghat. We paused to take in the view, and recalled how we had revelled at reaching that point on the outward march. We stopped for lunch halfway down in the shade of trees as it was roasting hot.

Dolalghat was celebrating Diwali, the Hindu Festival of Light, and most of the male population sat in groups by the wayside playing cards or throwing dice. We paused to buy bananas and a pineapple, and pushed on again over a swaying bridge across the Indrawati, the first really huge river on our route, and almost immediately over another swaying bridge across the Sun Kosi shortly before the rivers joined.

On the narrow track above the course of the Sun Kosi we met Narendra Saksena, one of three Indian journalists who shared control of all news from Kathmandu to the outside world. He greeted me as stringer for the *Daily Express* and opened a bottle of Danish beer for me, delicious despite being warm. He asked me to write a note to Countess Gravina recommending her to talk to him, but I refused. Besides working for the Indian English-language *Statesman* newspaper, I knew he worked for Reuters, and later I found my refusal was even more justified since he was working, despite his denials, for the *Daily Mail* under the name of Nicholas Saxon.

He told me he had left Kathmandu two days before, by Landrover to Banepa and had camped one night already and was camping that afternoon in Dolalghat.[2]

I pushed on for another hour before we found a place to camp on the edge of the river below the track, close by where I had bathed on the outward trek. It was a lovely spot with the river and woodlands, but the porters were not happy about it. They asked for more pills against malaria as soon as they dropped their loads,

---

[2] That's as far as he got; the 4,000-foot climb beyond was too much for him and he had to wait in Dolalghat for five days before the women arrived. That did not stop him sending a story largely based on my old cables to the *Daily Express*, datelined 'By runner from Risingo, 50 miles from Kathmandu', about the women arriving in a valley celebrating the Festival of Light which was already over when the women arrived there. Oddly, too, it didn't appear in the *Daily Mail* until a whole week later when the women were already back in Kathmandu. It must have been sheer torture for Saksena to get as far as Dolalghat lumbering along with the help of a thick staff. It struck me that he was the first fat man I had met in my travels on foot.

and all except one left to climb higher for the night. The lone porter who stayed had a jolly splash in the river himself after I had bathed. I wrote in my log, 'Last camp, thank God.'

For supper we ate the slender rations left, mutton with rice, greens and chapattis and bananas and pineapple for dessert, leaving just boiled eggs and bananas for breakfast. It was yet another wondrous starlit night with crickets chirping while we ate supper around a blazing camp fire, bigger than any before because of plentiful wood. Tired as I was, I felt reluctant to leave it and take to my sleeping bag. Next day I would be back in the world of wheeled transport and everything else, and I realised sadly that an adventure in the wilderness such as I had dreamed about as a boy was almost ended.

Saturday, October 31st: Risenko to Kathmandu

I was up before dawn, aiming to make Banepa by noon, having asked for transport to wait there from 11 a.m. There were lots of people on the trail, some old Ghurkhas snapping off smart salutes, others wanting to chat. We went rapidly over two clay ridges, and dropped down into the last broad valley before Banepa, reaching its far end under gruelling sun by 8.30 a.m. It was another lovely day, and the valley was smiling with vivid green paddy fields, huddles of houses where children played on swings and small roughly hewn versions of a Big Wheel, all made by loving parents to gladden the children's Diwali holiday. Crickets were chirping, wagtail birds hopped and flitted everywhere. We were back in a friendly world where the rigours of high altitude were unknown. Only Chowang had kept up my fast pace. Ratna and the porters were far behind.

That last long climb above that lush valley seemed never ending, struggling up one steep red clay slope after another, baked in the sun. At last we came to the last rocky valley before Banepa where the track climbed steeply across rock walls to the last ridge that hid the beginnings of the rough motor track. My rucksack was rubbing painfully, my legs ached with fatigue, but we went down the final ridge at a sprint towards the new corrugated roof, put on since we last passed, that marked the mission hospital. So fast, that we came near to treading on a cobra that wriggled across our path pursued by stone-throwing villagers. My spirits dropped when there was no sign of a waiting vehicle, for the last miles to Kathmandu seemed just too much.

At the top of the hill where the women had made their first camp and where I had slept in the temple on my first night on the trail to the mountains, I met a strange sight — a European-looking family, the man in a smart lightweight suit, a well-groomed woman in a summer dress and nylons with two toddlers in bright rompers. I asked them a silly question. Was there was a telephone in the village? The woman answered in an American drawl, 'Go ask Dr Sturgess. We're just visiting here.'

As I walked to Dr Sturgess's bungalow I noticed my trousers were rolled up above my knees, and I realised that I must have presented a strange figure, carrying an ice axe, to American visitors. I rolled my trousers down, and walked past the glass windows of a smart Western-designed bungalow, and paused at the sound of a piano and hymn singing. I waited till the hymn was finished and knocked on the door. Dr Sturgess, whom I had met briefly six weeks before, introduced me to his wife, to an Indian doctor and his wife, and a Canadian nurse, all visiting him. I sank gratefully into a soft, upholstered armchair in a room furnished according to Western style and a woman's taste, and there were Western toys on the carpet.

I wondered whether I thought these things were stranger to me than the apparition of a man suddenly appearing from the wilderness must have been to them. The glass of iced water tasted like champagne, and I was on my second when another visitor appeared at the front door, a genial, grey-haired man in a check sports jacket and flannels who had come out in a Landrover to meet me. He introduced himself as David Isaacs, a New Yorker with a touch of Cockney in his voice, and soon he was filming the arrival of my porters, and he got me to arrive again for the benefit of his film.

He had brought luncheon boxes and bottles of cold beer, and Chowang and I feasted while waiting for Ratna and the straggling line of porters to join us. Then the loads and porters were stowed in the back of the Landrover, and we bumped down the hill through the narrow main street of Banepa, past a lorry stuck in mud, and across Kathmandu valley to the city, and on to the Royal Hotel.

My fine Jumbesi porters dumped their loads on the balcony outside my hotel room. I paid them 60 rupees on the basis of a six-day march from Jumbesi instead of the three hard days we had done, and Chowang and Ratna took an advance and agreed to return for the balance next day.

In my mail was a rather dubious letter from the foreign editor telling me 'I think the coverage you have given us has been quite terrific apart from the scoop secured by the *Daily Mail* last Saturday morning which was not your fault.'

By that time lunch was being served, and I was hungry again despite the picnic at Banepa. Others at lunch in the plush, picture gallery, chandelier-hung dining room looked at me curiously as I took a table. My deep tan and trek-stained clothes were out of place among the crisp white tablecloths, napkins and white-gloved and liveried bearers who served a succession of courses.

It made a change from sitting on a rock with a plate on my knees and Chowang wiping the knife and fork on his soiled bush-shirt before handing them to me. Most of the others were American tourists, arrived that morning by plane to spend a couple of days photographing Nepal, and their interest increased as I heard the maître d'hôtel making the rounds telling every table that I had just walked in from Everest.

I had made Kathmandu from Namche Bazar in eight days, half the recognised light trekking time, and Colonel Roberts, who had trekked the route himself, told me later that I had set up a record for the journey unmatched by expedition climbers, easily the fastest time for the route by a European.

After 42 days in the wilderness it was a joy to wallow in my first hot bath, and throw out all my trekking clothing for the *dhobie*. A joy, too, to put on a white shirt and tie with a tropical suit to go to the Embassy for drinks that evening, and later to climb ecstatically between fresh white sheets in a real bed.

Chapter Ten

Return to Kathmandu

Six days after my return to Kathmandu I took two Landrovers to Banepa to meet the women who had begun the return trek later the same day that I had left Namche Bazar. They were all well, though Loulou Boulaz had sprained an ankle and walked with the aid of ski sticks. Riding on the last lap into the Nepalese capital, the women gaped at a cyclist, gasped at the sight of petrol pumps and a few motor cars. Kathmandu had changed even in the three months they had been away. Margaret Darvall said half-regretfully, 'City life again.'

It was dark when we reached the hotel where hotel-owner Boris was frantically making room in his 54-bed hotel, already swamped with tourists, for the new arrivals. He had hoped the women might camp in their tents on the hotel lawns and share one room for the use of a bath. But the porters with the tents were still far behind. So the seven women from Europe shared two rooms with bath and three beds. The Tenzing girls, who had been met at the end of the motor track by the Indian Ambassador, were staying again at his residence.

Countess Gravina was unperturbed. She said, 'We have a floor and a bath. That's enough to start with.' Eileen Healey said, 'A bath, wonderful. That will do for now.' While accommodation was being sorted out they drank beer and brandy and ate chicken sandwiches and pastries with great glee.

Only Pem-Pem Tensing was sad. With the expedition over, the full impact of Claudine's death hit her. She told me, 'Claudine was the best friend I've ever had. We shared a tent on the approach march and at Base Camp. She advised me on everything. She was going to stay with me at Darjeeling instead of going straight home from Kathmandu. Now everything seems so empty without her.'

That evening the women, bathed and, hair well brushed, put on dresses for the first time to attend a farewell dinner with me. The menu was cream of tomato soup, Eggs Florentine, Chicken Royale, fried new potatoes, braised carrots, purée of spinach, Diplomatic Pudding and coffee. Squeals of pleasure greeted each course.

It was my last meeting with them. My unique assignment was over and I flew back to London the next day.

Appendix One:
Background to Himalayan Climbing

Sir Francis Younghusband planned to explore the Everest region and climb the world's highest peak in 1893. But he was refused permission to enter Tibet. Nepal, the only Hindu monarchy, perched along the southern slopes of the central Himalaya for 480 miles, was closed to foreigners. Eight peaks towering over 26,250 feet could only be distantly viewed from the Indian frontier. Tibet, ruled by the Dalai Lama, revered as a living God, controlled the world's highest plateau on the northern side. It was even more isolated, by both geography and a deep antipathy towards foreigners.

The Great Trigonometrical Survey of India, under Surveyor-General George Everest, calculated from the Indian frontier in 1852 that a mountain they labelled Peak XV was the highest in the world. It was named Everest after the former Surveyor-General in 1865. It is still known to the Sherpa people who live at its foot as Chomo Lungma – Goddess Mother of the Land.

In 1904 the Viceroy of India, Lord Curzon, appointed Young-husband to establish a mission in Lhasa, the Tibetan capital. His escort fought stout resistance to reach Lhasa, but then had to withdraw. It was not until 1920 that the Dalai Lama gave permission for an expedition to enter Tibet and to attempt to scale Everest from the northern side. By that time the elderly Younghusband had become President of the Royal Geographical Society, and he sent George Leigh Mallory to survey the route in 1921. A year later the first Everest expedition set out from the Indian resort town of Darjeeling, crossed neighbouring Sikkim into Tibet, and set up a Base Camp near the Rongbuk Monastery at the foot of Everest. Several of its members reached 27,000 feet before the expedition had to be abandoned when bad weather caused the loss of seven porters in avalanches.

During the next expedition in 1924 George Mallory and his

climbing companion Andrew Irvine were seen to have reached the last stretch just below the summit when cloud obscured them and they were never seen again.[1]

For the next eight years the Dalai Lama refused permission for expeditions because of bad signs in the horoscopes. Expeditions were permitted in 1933, in 1936 and in 1938 but all failed to reach the summit. After the Second World War the present Dalai Lama, then a child, refused permission because the horoscope was again 'unpropitious'. Then the Chinese occupation closed Tibet to foreigners.

An approach through Nepal became feasible in 1949 when the Rana family, rulers of Nepal as hereditary Prime Ministers since 1852, were ousted from power by the King whom they had kept under palace arrest. Nepal slowly opened up to the outside world.

An Anglo-American expedition trekked through Nepal to survey the southern slopes of Everest in 1950, and in 1951 a group of British climbers took a closer look. They marked out the route for a 200-mile trek over 17 lateral ranges that separated lush monsoon-nurtured valleys. This route, with established overnight stopping places, was followed by all later expeditions to the Sherpa region around Everest. It passed through occasional small villages with rice paddies and pasture where water buffalo grazed in the valleys, and terraces growing millet, buckwheat, maize and barley reached up to 8,000 feet. In the higher valleys sheep and yaks seasonally grazed up to 15,000 feet amid luxuriant forests with magnificent cedars, giant rhododendrons and bamboo thickets. Higher still were larch, birch and stunted bush rhododendrons.

A first Swiss Everest expedition nearly stole a march on British ambitions to be first on top of the world. They obtained exclusive permission for the 1952 season. Its leader, famed Alpinist Raymond Lambert, accompanied by a Sherpa named Tenzing Norgay, reached 27,000 feet before abandoning their attempt. They blamed their failure to reach the summit on not taking sufficient time for full acclimatisation before making the summit attempt.

That same year, in preparation for the full-scale British attempt on Everest the next year, Eric Shipton led an Everest training party that included Edmund Hillary to a practice climb on Cho Oyu

---

[1] In May, 1999 an American expedition found a body which proved to be Mallory. This led to speculation that disaster struck them on their way down after reaching the summit.

(26,750 feet). This was to try out young climbers, study monsoon weather conditions and test oxygen equipment. Bad weather around Cho Oyu forced them to turn back as they reached a 250-foot ice cliff at 22,500 feet.

Hillary and Sherpa Tenzing Norgay took part in the British 1953 Everest expedition and reached the summit roped together. News of this long-awaited success reached London on Queen Elizabeth II's Coronation Day, headlined as the 'crowning glory'.

Appendix Two:
Other Women High Climbers

Women have shared the allure of mountain climbing, its rigours and risks, from the time when the first climbers were botanists in the mid-nineteenth century.

Mlle Henriette D'Angeville, a survivor of the French aristocracy, was the first woman to climb Mont Blanc, the highest peak in Europe, in 1838, but it was not until 1854 that the first English-woman, a Mrs Hamilton, reached the Mont Blanc summit, climbing with her husband and guides. Another English woman, Lucy Walker, was the first woman to stand on the Matterhorn summit in 1871. That was six years after three members of a British male party who scaled it were killed while descending. Lucy Walker later became President of the Ladies Alpine Club, founded in 1907.

The Cho Oyu women's claim to be the first all-woman expedition to the Himalayas overlooked a smaller all-woman expedition by three members of the Ladies Scottish Climbing Club in May 1955. They were the first to reach the summit of 21,898-foot Mount Gyalgen in the Jugal Himal, the nearest peak to the north of Kathmandu. The story of that climb was published by Collins in 1956 under the title, *Tents in the Clouds: the First Women's Himalayan Expedition.*

Monica Jackson, co-author, wrote in a prologue, 'In the Spring of 1955, three of us, mountaineers with no claim to fame, became the first expedition composed entirely of women ever to explore and climb in the high Himalayas. Several women had already climbed in the Himalayas, and the significance of the fact that they had all done so as members of expeditions planned and led by men escaped us entirely at first.'

The other women in this modest expedition were Elizabeth Stark and Evelyn Camrass. Mrs Jackson recorded, 'We succeeded in doing all we hoped to do.'

After the tragic loss of two women and two Sherpas on Cho Oyu in 1959, as described in this book, nearly a decade passed before the next all-woman expedition challenged one of the major Himalayan peaks. A Japanese all-woman expedition climbed a peak called Putha Hiunchuli (23,774 feet), first climbed by Colonel Jimmy Roberts and Sherpa Ang Nyima, in the Annapurna Range of Western Nepal. One of the women climbers and a Sherpa were killed in an avalanche, and another woman climber died at Base Camp.

A woman was included in an Everest expedition for the first time in 1972. She was the Swiss Yvette Vaucher, whose husband was also in the expedition. There was a move for Yvette to be among those to make a summit attempt, and make her the first woman to reach the top of the world, but the expedition was dogged by adverse weather and nothing came of it.

Three years later, in 1975, a Japanese all-woman expedition climbed Everest; its leader Junko Tabei, was the first woman to stand on its summit. That year China also claimed that a nine-woman team had reached the Everest summit.

Vera Komarkova, an American born in what is now the Czech Republic, reached the summit of Annapurna (26,504 feet) in the autumn of 1978. She was a member of an American expedition made up of ten women climbers, two film-makers and a Base Camp manager. They employed 217 Sherpa and Sherpani porters. In a second assault two of them, roped together, fell to their deaths. In 1984 Komarkova was the first woman to set foot on the summit of Cho Oyu.

In 1989 an eight-member British Women's Expedition climbed the sharp-edged pyramid of Gasherbrum 11 (26,360 feet, 8,035 metres) in the Karakorams without Sherpas or oxygen, truly an all-woman expedition. Its leader, Rhona Lampard, echoed the women of Cho Oyu. When she told a *Times* reporter 'The point of being in an all-woman expedition was that no-one could say oh well they just got taken up it. Women go on mixed expeditions and reach summits, but there's always a feeling, the men probably did all the hard work.'

In May 1993 Rebecca Stephens, 31, who had earlier climbed to 23,000 feet as a reporter covering a 1989 Anglo-American expedition on the north-east ridge of Everest, became the first British woman to reach the Everest summit. Alison Hargeaves, a Derbyshire mother of two, became the first woman and the second person to climb Everest solo without oxygen, in May 1995. Just a month later, with two other climbers she reached the summit of K2 (28,244 feet), the second highest mountain, again without oxygen. She died when overcome by a fierce storm during the descent. Julie Tillis, the first and only other British woman to climb K2, died from hypothermia when caught in storms during the descent.

During 2004–5 a 36-year-old London estate agent, Annabelle Bond, climbed the highest mountains in the seven continents, totalling 150,000 feet, in 360 days, halving the previous record by the previous fastest woman and the fourth fastest since this supreme mountaineering competition began a few years ago. The seven summits were Everest on the Nepal/Tibet border (8,850 metres), Aconcagua on the Argentine/Chile border (6,962 m), Mt Denali also known as Mt McKinley in Alaska (6,194 m), Kilimanjaro in Africa (5,895 m), Elbrus in Russia (5.642 m), Vinson in Antarctica (4,897 m) and Kosciusko in Australia (2,228 m). Her climbs raised more than £800,000 for an Eve appeal ovarian cancer charity.

Easy access provided by building roads and small airfields have opened the Everest area to tourists during the last several decades, and well over a thousand people have now stood on the world's highest peak. Climbing Everest led to comparatively few fatalities, compared with the first ascent of K2 in 1954 on which there have since been 37 deaths in 113 ascents of a peak notoriously difficult to climb.

Dr Andrew Sutherland, who reached the Everest summit in May, 2006 was shocked at the deaths of fifteen climbers on Everest during the year till then. One in ten of those who reached the summit died on the way down, mainly due to altitude-related illnesses.

Appendix Three:
Altitude Sickness

Years after the 1953 Everest expedition, one of its members, Dr Michael Ward, published a paper on research into altitude sickness which he carried out for the Mount Everest Foundation. His findings showed that high-altitude mountaineering may be unacceptably dangerous to all but a few super-fit humans. The air pressure at the summit of Everest is about one-third of sea-level pressure, making it so much harder for a climber to fill his lungs with the oxygen necessary for energy, to fend off frostbite and hypothermia, and to prevent degeneration of particularly sensitive areas of the brain.

Dr Ward noted, 'If you do not have enough oxygen you cannot work properly. You cannot produce the heat needed and your body begins to cool down so that you suffer frostbite even though you are still moving. It may be that Mallory and Irving, and Boardman and Tasker [who disappeared high on Everest in 1982] were simply overwhelmed by cold. Lack of oxygen caused their loss rather than a fall.'

Andrew Peacock, an expert on medical effects of high altitude who climbed to 26,000 feet with Rebecca Stephens in May 1993, believed that she and others able to carry on to the high summits must have had what he called a 'blunted reflex in the lungs' that permits their bodies to react more slowly to the effects of lack of oxygen. He reported, 'I was far gone at 26,000 but Rebecca was able to continue. Of the four of us she was in the best shape.'